The
Dilemmas
of
Family
Wealth

Also available from
BLOOMBERG PRESS

Family Wealth—Keeping It in the Family:
How Family Members and Their Advisers Preserve Human,
Intellectual, and Financial Assets for Generations
by James E. Hughes Jr.

Managing Concentrated Stock Wealth:
An Adviser's Guide to Building Customized Solutions
by Tim Kochis

The PPLI Solution:
Delivering Wealth Accumulation, Tax Efficiency, and Asset
Protection Through Private Placement Life Insurance
edited by Kirk Loury

Tax-Aware Investment Management:
The Essential Guide
by Douglas S. Rogers, CFA

A complete list of our titles is available at
www.bloomberg.com/books

The
Dilemmas
of
Family
Wealth

INSIGHTS ON
SUCCESSION, COHESION, AND LEGACY

BY

JUDY MARTEL

WITH A FOREWORD BY JAMES E. HUGHES JR.

BLOOMBERG PRESS
NEW YORK

BLOOMBERG, BLOOMBERG LEGAL, *BLOOMBERG MARKETS,* BLOOMBERG NEWS, BLOOMBERG PRESS, BLOOMBERG PROFESSIONAL, BLOOMBERG RADIO, BLOOMBERG TELEVISION, BLOOMBERG TERMINAL, and BLOOMBERG TRADEBOOK are trademarks and service marks of Bloomberg L.P. All rights reserved.

Certified Financial Planner Board of Standards Inc. owns the certification marks CFP® and CERTIFIED FINANCIAL PLANNER™.

This publication contains the author's opinions and is designed to provide accurate and authoritative information. It is sold with the understanding that the author, publisher, and Bloomberg L.P. are not engaged in rendering legal, accounting, investment-planning, estate-planning, or other professional advice. The reader should seek the services of a qualified professional for such advice; the author, publisher, and Bloomberg L.P. cannot be held responsible for any loss incurred as a result of specific investments or planning decisions made by the reader.

Editor's note: Some of the families in this book who did not wish to be identified by name also requested that a few details about their families be changed to protect their identity. The experiences that such families are relating for the purposes of illustrating dilemmas they faced, however, have not been changed.

Portions of chapters one and two were developed from material that appeared in articles by the author in *Worth* magazine in December 2004. Portions of chapter five appeared in articles by the author in *Worth* in March and April 2004 and in March 2005.

First Edition published 2006
1 3 5 7 9 10 8 6 4 2

Library of Congress Cataloging-in-Publication Data

Martel, Judy
    The dilemmas of family wealth : insights on succession, cohesion, and legacy / by Judy Martel ; with a foreword by James E. Hughes Jr.
        p. cm
    Summary: "Drawing on the experiences of real families and of leading professionals, the author offers guidance for members of extended families and their advisers on dealing with the financial and nonfinancial challenges of significant wealth. Topics include effective family governance, preservation of human and intellectual capital, instilling appropriate values in children, wise inheritance planning, and managing intergenerational conflicts"--Provided by publisher.
    Includes index.
    ISBN 1-57660-190-0 (alk. paper)
    1. Finance, Personal--United States. 2. Family--Economic aspects--United States. 3. Estate planning--United States. 4. Inheritance and succession--United States. 5. Communication in the family--United States. I. Title.

HG179.M3423 2006
332.024--dc22   2005035446

*To the many families who readily shared their
personal stories with me, and without whom
this book would not have been possible*

To Jay Hughes, for his enthusiasm and gentle advice

*To Jared Kieling and Bob Casey,
for their guidance and patience*

*And to my husband, Bob, always,
for his loving support*

Contents

Part One: Transitions and Letting Go
Introduction   34

Dilemma: It's time to plan for succession, but I don't know how to let go of the business.

Dilemma: I sold my business at the right time and have more than enough to take care of my family, but I feel alone and uncomfortable in my new position of wealth. What do I do with my time, and how do I preserve a connection with the family wealth in subsequent generations?

Dilemma: As the family grows, the original fortune is not enough to support everyone. How can I support and encourage future wealth generators to add to the family coffers?

Part Two: Retaining Family Cohesiveness
Introduction   90

Dilemma: I want the wealth to enhance our dreams, but don't want it to be the only reason we stay together.

FOREWORD

It is both an honor and privilege to write the foreword to Judy Martel's book *The Dilemmas of Family Wealth*. As I begin this work, two quotations come to mind: Churchill's description of Stalin as "an enigma wrapped in a paradox" and Santayana's statement that "those who fail to study history are condemned to repeat it." A book on human and family dilemmas suggests that underlying the issues posed by the predicaments must be deeper fundamental issues of human behavior that cause these dilemmas to emerge in the first place. Equally, their successful resolution must be based on time-tested behaviors that can be discovered, as Judy Martel has done, through the wisdom that comes from studying the experiences of others who have faced similar situations.

In the case of the dilemmas posed here, I believe the underlying issues that cause them are a set of paradoxes in family behavior that replicate Churchill's enigmas [dilemmas] wrapped in paradox. Similarly, because some of the paradoxes of human behavior in families have been described in writings as old as our earliest written texts, Santayana's admonition comes home to roost if we fail to study the history of human behavior they recount.

The first and most profound human behavior underlying the dilemmas is described in the proverb "shirtsleeves to shirtsleeves in three generations." In my lifelong journey studying and serving families with financial wealth, I discovered early on that this proverb is culturally universal. Sometimes it is expressed as "clogs to clogs," as "rags to riches to rags," as "rice paddy to rice paddy," and on and on, depending on the culture trying to express it. In all its forms, it describes a process of the creation of a financial fortune in the first generation, the plateau or stasis of that family's financial growth in the second generation, and the consumption of the family fortune in the third, with the fourth generation back in the "rice paddy" pulling rice. The proverb sadly offers only a negative prophesy with no hope for a family's reprieve from its profoundly depreciated outcome.

In my studies and observations of hundreds of families, I have learned that this proverb is not only universal, but it is also as old as writing itself. It is likely, therefore, that it is *prehistoric* since I don't believe human behavior changed just because someone began describing it in writing.

The proverb expresses, in its negativity regarding a family's ability to maintain its financial capital for more than three generations, a universal law of modern physics—the second law of thermodynamics, or the law of entropy. In physics we know that all matter materializes from the energy that forms the universe and that it will undergo the process of friction and decay, called entropy, as the material gradually returns to energy. Of course, this can occur spontaneously as fission and wipe out the material in an instant. This can also happen to the materiality of families. But through the process of fusion, this process might be suspended indefinitely, a very nice thought for families seeking to avoid the effects of the law of entropy as expressed in the proverb.

The law of entropy as it applies to families, as with all other forms of energy, is immutable, but it says nothing about how many generations of a family may live and die before it comes true. For this reason, free will enters the picture. It is true that every family's destiny is to eventually disappear, as entropy predicts, but nothing says when. Herein lies every family's choice and the dilemmas Judy Martel describes help us make many positive choices as we seek to resolve them.

Our negative proverb expresses the law of entropy as it applies to the life cycle of a family's financial capital. It describes the materialization of financial capital through the creativity of the first generation, its plateau in the second generation as the creative energy dissipates, and then the friction or entropy of consumption in the third, with the energy of the financial capital fully dissipated by the fourth.

The laws of physics and the universality of human experience make competing with the proverb's verdict regarding the ability of a family to maintain its financial capital for more then three generations highly unlikely. Yet, there are families who succeed. Why and how do they do it?

I suggest that it is through a long sequence of linked transitions in which each succeeding generation seeks to find and replicate the creativity of the first generation. Each member of the subsequent generations does so by discovering his "work" as calling—not necessarily having anything to do with wages—and mastering it. In this way, each person becomes as fully self-aware, individuated, free, and awakened as possible. Then, by applying what they learn together toward dynamically stewarding and conserving the wealth as great second-generation members so that the capital never plateaus, the family never reaches the predicted third-generation reality of financial dissipation, reflected in lives that are unrealized and unaware. Families seeking to work through and live out the process successfully create systems to enhance their joint decision-making so that each succeeding generation can together make the horizontal social compact necessary to govern itself and avoid the result the proverb prophecies.

What are some of the issues families must concern themselves with when creating such governance systems? They must (a) discover who makes up their family systems of affinity and (b) they must understand family systems theory concerning how families actually operate in increasingly complex structures of decision-making as their demography naturally increases and decreases.

Failure to know who actually is a family of affinity member and how that person engages in the family decision-making process dooms a family to the chaos that always ensues when any system cannot gently and naturally evolve to higher levels of complexity. When a family system does not appreciate its nature and, therefore, cannot maintain its natural order when it is shedding its skin to grow larger and deal with more difficult issues, it will fail. A further problem for families in understanding their systems lies in defining who is in a family of affinity. All too often the family defines itself too narrowly, leaving out its mentoring trustees and its *personnes de confiance,* thereby excluding from its decision-making process some of its greatest resources and wisdom on how great families come to be and what processes they employed to achieve and maintain that status.

Families must be able to recognize the transitions they are in if they are to understand where and how they are currently at risk for the proverb's entropic prophesy. If a family is to reach its fourth and fifth generation in good shape, and go on from there (my definition of a great or successful family), the first thing it must do is imagine that it is in a 200-year process. Why 200 years? Well, given modern life expectancy, it will take at least a century for the third generation to be born and die, and if we add the fourth and fifth generation, to ensure that we really have a system of joint decision-making that is avoiding the effect of the proverb, we quickly reach a 200-year horizon. As soon as we begin to think this way, we see that no current transaction—financial or otherwise—is likely to be critical to the outcome of the family journey provided we approach every decision as second-generation dynamic steward-conservators seeking to bring creativity to our long-term decisions. What we need to do is bring to our 200-year process some time-tested tools for making good joint decisions. The best tools I know are the following:

First is my father's admonition "where is the beginning?" All too often, families don't take the time to think through where their current transition really began and what the characteristics of the transition are. Equally important, they often fail to perceive that a new transition hasn't begun just because a new generation may have reached adulthood. And even more often, they fail to perceive when a transition ends and waste valuable time beginning the "new" instead of fully closing out the "old," thus burdening the new with unfinished business that constantly creeps into the new's progress and stifles it. Families can gain much positive ground avoiding the proverb's effects if they study themselves in light of the proverb as organic entities in order to know where in the life cycle of the generations they are and the transitions these stages represent, and then by applying their joint decision-making to that reality.

Second, families must do "Seventh Generation Thinking," following the wisdom of the Iroquois elder who begins every tribal gathering of this now over six-hundred-year-old family of affinity with the admonition "Let us hope that the decisions we make today will be honored by our tribal members seven generations from today." This is perhaps the best tool I have ever encountered for long-term family success.

Third is "hasten slowly." Time is a family's best friend in 200-year transitional thinking. But as with all friends, treat them with great kindness and do not waste their gifts. Fourth and finally, remember that it is the Tortoise who wins long races and the Hare who runs out of gas.

When families understand their systems and their transitions as they seek to govern themselves well toward reaching their fifth generations in good shape, and to go on from there, what are likely to be the most difficult issues for them to contend with?

I have come to believe that they constitute a group of paradoxes. Paradoxes because the thinking about each such issue, and the generally accepted answer, bring about the proverb's success, with all the human suffering entailed, while it is a family acting in the opposite way that offers some possibility for a more positive outcome. What then are these paradoxes that are reflected in and underlie Martel's dilemmas?

First, the wealth of a family that is critical to its long-term success are its human and intellectual capitals as reflected in the levels of the thriving of its members, their levels of self-awareness, and their competencies. Financial capital can help grow these other two capitals, but on its own (or worse, as a family's principal focus), financial capital can do little more than bring on the effects of the proverb.

All dynamic enterprises are a combination of the human beings who form them (their human capital); of the knowledge that these people have; of their capacity to learn, experience, and integrate new ideas (their intellectual capital); and lastly of their financial capital as a tool for growing the first two. Paradoxically, all family leaders know this to be true in every enterprise, other than their families. By forgetting this truth where their families are concerned, all the while without seeing that it is the growth of the family's human and intellectual capitals as in every dynamic enterprise that really matters, and concentrating their efforts on growing the family's financial capital, those leaders allow the proverb to work its stealthy will.

Second, families who see themselves as people with affinity, rather than as people with common blood, open their family systems to new energy. They do not close their systems and block the new energy that every generation needs to balance what they will naturally lose. Perhaps the greatest fallacy families can fall into is to define themselves as blood, when in reality, no family has ever existed that did not begin with two people with an affinity. In fact, there has never been a family of blood! The creation myth of every culture recognizes this and defines its founding through the affinity of two people. Woe to the family that defines away reality in favor of the hubris of defining its blood as something special. Why? Because its creation myth begins with a fallacy from which it is nearly impossible to escape the consequences of the proverb. The proverb is daunting enough. A family needn't begin its fight to overcome it from a false reality.

This paradox of how families define themselves lies at the heart of the failure of many families. No family ever has enough human and intellectual capital, just as no enterprise of any sort ever has enough of these. What we know about combating the proverb is that the most successful enterprises, and families are enterprises, are the most open and welcoming to additions of these critical capitals. They are systems of affinity. At some level, all unsuccessful enterprises represent closed unwelcoming systems that are unable to add the new sources of human and intellectual capital they need to remain dynamic.

Third, family systems that say "do this for us and we might do something for you" are doomed to fail, whereas those that say "what can we do to *enhance* your individual journey toward the dynamic preservation of our family as a whole," before asking anything of you, succeed. Every human being I have met, even those most empty of spirit, has sought to find a group that will promote the growth within him to a higher level of freedom and self-awareness. To reach their fifth generations and go on from there, families must remain positively attracted to all potential new members. Family systems that enslave by obligation to the system first, and with some possible benefits later, are negatively attracting and will drive away potential members. Family systems that seek to enhance the individual journey of each member are founded on the growth of individual freedom and, as such, are more positively attracting than their opposites. Paradoxically, most families' systems of governance start with obligation and duty instead of with individual members' journeys, dreams, and passions, and thereby contribute from inception to the proverb's success as they fail to acknowledge the real needs of their members. Founding a family's vision and mission around individual members' enhancement toward the dynamic preservation of the family as a whole works toward success because it is energizing to its members and to their life goals of achieving individual freedom and greater self-awareness.

Fourth, learning to become a great strategic owner of a family's financial capital is an art critical to the dynamic preservation of a family's wealth, whereas management is a science to carry out the owner's strategic vision. All families with significant financial capital are at risk of the paradox that it is ownership, rather than management, that matters to a family's long-term success. That management, while a primary tool, is only one of the tactical tools a family needs to achieve success. How many families spend endless hours on management succession (often with deep wounding of the family's social compact as invidious choices among equals tear at the family's fabric of relationships) while spending no time on teaching all members to become strategic owners? Only then to discover that when the really critical issues in the transitions of their enterprises require the owners to make great joint decisions that the owners have no experience of being owners and make entropic decisions as a result? Management succession is important but, paradoxically, no management can manage successfully if the owner's vision isn't guiding the work. Absentee owners, which is what uneducated owners are, may stroke management's ego as the owners leave management free rein to follow its own way, but this drives family enterprises into entropy, with the resulting dissipation of the family's financial capital.

In my experience, when addressing financial capital issues, families need to spend 90 percent of their time learning to be great owners (what I define as dynamic steward-conservators) and 10 percent on management succession, if they are to be successful dynamic steward-conservators. Why? Because one cannot choose the right manager if one doesn't fully comprehend all of the strategic issues the enterprise faces going forward.

Fifth, in every generation after the first, the critical leader needed for excellent family joint decision-making is the leader from behind rather than the leader from in front. Families, from their second generation on, are communities of people with equal genealogical linkage to the first family couple of affinity. Each individual family member, regardless of his or her share of the family's financial capital, has an equal claim to leadership and to its glue—its stories.

In a family seeking to enhance the individual journey of each of its members toward the dynamic preservation of the family as a whole, each individual member seeks attention from the family's leadership to achieve success on his journey. This necessitates individual guidance—a system of leadership that is quintessentially from behind.

Conversely, if the family's leaders are directing from in front, it is natural that *their* individual goals will be paramount, as they seek followers to achieve them, with a concomitant disregard for the individual journeys of each of their followers. Specialists in the field generally do not teach leadership from behind, but it is the only form of leadership I have discovered that actually works in families, given the natural equality of family members.

Again this reality expresses paradox because it is leadership from in front that most families practice. In doing so, families allow the proverb to come true as the growth of the human and intellectual capital of each family member is substituted by the entropic obligations and duties required of family members by the leader in order for the leader to achieve his goals. The proverb subtly works its will.

Each of the five paradoxes lies at the root of a family's failure to thrive and each in its own way produces the dilemmas that this book describes. In seeking to solve these dilemmas, if families can bring an awareness of these paradoxes of behavior, combined with a knowledge of their family's system and the transitions in their family in which these systems are operating, all toward governing themselves in a more enlightened fashion, they are likely to find solutions to these dilemmas that increase their well-being and equally reduce the suffering of those they love the most by the care and attention they give to their resolution.

We are blessed that Judy Martel has seen fit to bring these dilemmas to our attention. We can benefit those we love the most by deeply engaging with each of their resolutions, aimed at reducing human suffering, and most importantly, growing great families governing themselves toward the long-term realization of their members' dreams and away from the proverb's pernicious prognosis.

James E. Hughes Jr.
Author of *Family Wealth:*
Keeping It in the Family

The

Dilemmas
of
Family
Wealth

INTRODUCTION

Images of wealth planning typically conjure up the serious faces of outsiders—attorneys, accountants, and investment advisers all devising techniques to increase financial riches—resulting in complicated trusts and sophisticated investments that allow for the eventual purchase of the 36-room mansion or the 50-foot yacht.

What is most likely lacking in these grand visions is, ironically, the most important component of preserving and growing wealth for generations to come: a common understanding and mutual acceptance of a family's values and an understanding of the dilemmas that are a hindrance to sustaining wealth. Sobering statistics point to the fact that when a family doesn't pay attention to itself, individual family members squander the financial capital—often in a single generation.

Author and generational wealth consultant Roy Williams says that of the 3,250 wealthy families he has studied over a 10-year period, 70 percent failed to successfully transfer wealth from one generation to the next, and in only 3 percent of those cases was the cause poor investments or lack of estate planning. In most cases, it was a deficiency of trust and communication among family members, leading to poor preparation of heirs.

Every family owns three forms of capital, and most people easily grasp the concept of financial capital, which consists of hard assets they can point to—property, securities, cash, and so on. Yet many families don't understand that their most precious forms of capital are the human (the members of the family) and the intellectual (the family's knowledge). The three forms of a family's capital are intertwined. The well-being of family members, working toward a common goal of success for each individual and for the family as a whole, will be enhanced by the knowledge its members cultivate.

From the start, a wealth creator's intellectual capital breeds his success in amassing financial capital. Thereafter, the human capital of the family must continue to be developed to sustain unity and harmony, leading to the acquisition of more intellectual capital. This cycle helps the family grow and retain its financial wealth. If the family fails to sustain its human and intellectual capital, the financial capital usually plummets. As we will see in Part III of this book, failure to prepare and educate heirs about money—which is essentially paying attention to the human and intellectual aspects of a family's capital—can have disastrous results. Heirs with little or no connection to how the money was earned will likely either adopt an attitude of fear toward the wealth or use it to satisfy their individual whims. In either case, the wealth will be wasted.

When a family understands its common purpose, members begin to build a legacy that is inclusive and supportive of individual as well as family goals, further strengthening the unit. If a family's human and intellectual capital fail to grow with each successive generation, an individual's primal urge to "take the money and run" will surface, and chances are, the money will rapidly disappear.

In David McCullough's book, *John Adams,* the author cites a letter written by the second president of the United States that sums up a sentiment for how each generation supports the next in its goals: "I must study politics and war that my sons may have liberty to study mathematics and philosophy. My sons ought to study mathematics and philosophy, geography, natural history, naval architecture, navigation, commerce, and agriculture in order to give their children a right to study paintings, poetry, music, architecture, statuary, tapestry and porcelain."

James (Jay) Hughes, retired trusts and estates attorney and consultant, interprets the quote by noting further that in wealthy families, the financial capital should be viewed as a tool to support the human and intellectual capital of its members. As the family improves and prospers as a unit and as individuals, the wealth will likely continue to enrich the family for generations because the family will be unified in its goals.

Successful families are those whose members understand that

preserving the family is a precursor to preserving the wealth, and there are countless success stories of family businesses that have seeded a notable family heritage. The chronicles that are offered for public critique are often those in which the family has struggled to assimilate the wealth into the lives of its members, and has ultimately squandered both its financial and human resources. In virtually every example of a family's financial failure, there is a corroborating story of its dysfunction.

According to Henry (Hap) Perry, founder and chairman of Asset Management Advisors (AMA), money acts as a magnifier. It can fuel great deeds that will enrich the family and society for generations or it can bring out the worst in people, tearing families apart and leaving an unfavorable legacy. The power of money makes it both easier and more difficult for a family to cultivate its human and intellectual capital. Easier because wealth gives family members the opportunity to help one another to achieve greatness. More difficult because selfishness and self-indulgence can drive family members, and the family itself, off track. Families must work hard to reduce the negative effects of great wealth and strive for the greater good.

The power of money to enhance, or distort, a family's destiny plays itself out as each generation deals with the opportunities and the burdens of wealth, and these easy-yet-difficult decisions are the dilemmas of family wealth that can imperil all three forms of a family's capital. Dilemmas are particularly vexing because they force difficult choices between two outcomes. Make the wrong choice and the family collapses. The goal of recognizing and understanding dilemmas is to prevent the blessings of family wealth from turning into the family curse. The family's blessing is its financial capital. But when a family chooses to focus on that alone, it ignores the curse—the unintended consequence of losing its human and intellectual capital through its own actions.

The proverb "from rags to riches to rags in three generations" grew out of examples of families who failed to recognize and overcome these dilemmas. That failure is repeated time and again in families who build wealth, only to lose it within two generations.

Eight Major Dilemmas

The eight major dilemmas that can bring down a family and its fortune are listed here:

1) It's time to plan for succession, but I don't know how to let go of the business.

2) I sold my business at the right time and have more than enough to take care of my family, but I feel alone and uncomfortable in my new position of wealth. What do I do with my time, and how do I preserve a connection with the family wealth in subsequent generations?

3) As the family grows, the original fortune is not enough to support everyone. How can I support and encourage future wealth generators to add to the family coffers?

4) I want the wealth to enhance our dreams, but don't want it to be the only reason we stay together.

5) As new members come into the clan through marriage, how do I level the playing field if one partner is less wealthy, and what value do certain structures like prenuptial agreements offer me?

6) I need to prepare my children and grandchildren for the responsibility of wealth, but I'm afraid that if they know too much, it will destroy any initiative to earn a living. How do I communicate this concern?

7) I plan to be fair to my children, but if I leave them unequal amounts of money, am I setting up a future battleground?

8) I want to give some of my wealth back to society, but how can I do it without my children thinking I've given away their inheritance, and in a manner that will reflect our values and enhance the family legacy?

Although the outcomes of these eight dilemmas may seem obvious, the solutions can be tricky. For example, most people know that if they give their children too much money, they probably destroy their children's initiative to work, and when a family has $100 million or more, the challenge becomes even greater because there is potentially more money to give. Although the founder of the family fortune may intend to leave his wealth to his offspring, how can he do so in a way that prevents a young adult (age 18 or 21, the age of majority in most states) from turning into a trust-fund baby?

In fact, the complex duality of dilemmas has enthralled human-kind through centuries of storytelling. Most often, the toughest choices are those that seem to offer immediate gratification for an individual versus the future greater good for the many. A peek into Greek and Roman mythology presents gripping examples of agonizing choices that result in both good and bad outcomes. One such example is the dilemma faced by Agamemnon, commander in chief of a coalition headed for Troy to rescue the famously beautiful Helen. Agamemnon learns that he must sacrifice his daughter, Iphigenia, in order to free his fleet from the unfavorable winds that have them trapped in the port of Aulis. In the play, *Iphigenia at Aulis* by Euripides, Agamemnon laments "'Tis terrible for me to bring myself to this, nor less terrible it is to refuse." Agamemnon decides to sacrifice his daughter for what he perceives is the greater good, but he suffers tremendous torment in reaching that conclusion.

A more recent example is in William Styron's novel, *Sophie's Choice,* in which a mother is forced to make the ultimate choice between her two children. A Nazi official in a concentration camp orders her to choose which of her two children will live. If she chooses neither, both will be killed. In making this horrific decision, she will be able to save at least one of them.

The dilemmas presented by the acquisition of great wealth today impart their own set of difficult choices—less dramatic certainly, but deeply worrisome for families who want to preserve and enhance both their hard-earned wealth and their clan's harmony and unity for future generations. In preparing subsequent generations to be responsible stewards of the wealth, the ultimate good for the family sometimes means not giving in to immediate gratification on the part of those individual members who are eyeing the latest sports car.

Let's take another example. The first dilemma addressed in this book involves the founder of the family fortune. After sacrificing to build and nurture the source of the wealth, he must at some point exit and let the next generation implement its own ideas and achieve its dreams. The dilemma is that in order to enhance the family and its future wealth, fresh ideas and approaches are necessary. As Jay Hughes points out, the next generation must be allowed to fulfill its own dreams. Yet the immediate concern is a new and significant role for the founder. It is up to the entire family to help guide the transition, although the founder is the one who must ultimately learn to let go.

The eight dilemmas featured in this book were chosen because they are the ones that wealthy families typically face as they move from generation to generation, according to wealth counselors, attorneys, and advisers. These issues are also the most critical because they intertwine every generation in a tangle of emotion and deeply held beliefs. It's never *just* about the money.

The first dilemma, as previously described, involves trust on the part of the founder—trusting the next generation to step up to the plate, take over his dream and life's work, and continue the family's success. The next generation has to trust that its dreams will take hold and prosper, thus enabling the family to retain the former success while possibly expanding into new areas of growth. This second generation also has to trust that the founder, who often anoints the successor, is not playing favorites, thus fueling existing sibling rivalries. Meanwhile, the founder's spouse trusts him to take her feelings into account.

The dilemma is further complicated by the points of view of the different generations involved. The founder may see his transition very differently from that of the rest of the family, setting up tension if the various sides cannot come to resolution.

The dilemmas presented in the chapters of this book progress in an order that begins with the founder of the wealth and continues through the second and third generations and beyond. Each dilemma is illustrated through the stories of families who are grappling with and, in some cases, solving it. Additional advice and solutions from wealth counselors and advisers who are trained to work with families are offered to find solutions to these dilemmas.

Identifying the Challenges

Following is a brief description of the main points of each chapter.

Chapter 1: It's time to plan for succession, but I don't know how to let go of the business. In some ways, the founder of the family business is ready to enjoy the fruits of his labors. But at the same time, he may not be prepared to assume a different role in the family and business structure.

- *Failing to transition:* Most businesses don't make a successful changeover from one generation to the next. Often, the first generation's reluctance shows up in a succession plan that is vague or not directly stated. Miscommunication or no communication hampers the plan and the progress of the family business.
- *Choosing a successor:* The selection should not rest solely on the shoulders of the founder. Those who retain the choice as theirs alone sometimes set themselves up for resentment and sibling rivalry. When the next generation is involved in choosing the successor—and perceives the choice as being an objective one—the odds for success increase.
- *Aiding the succession:* The first and second generations can work together to ensure that the business transitions successfully. The second generation usually consists of those who want to be directly involved in the business and those who want little involvement, but who wish to retain voting rights. If a plan is imposed on them by the previous generation, chances are great that it will be rejected.
- *Going public:* Sometimes the family must relinquish its full control and move to outside leadership. Changes to the business profile must be reflected in the family's goals and expectations for how the business will continue. The family must also work to expand opportunities for the rising generation, which may not be part of the public venture.

Chapter 2: I sold my business at the right time and have more than enough to take care of my family, but I feel alone and uncomfortable in my new position of wealth. What do I do with my time, and how do I preserve a connection with the family wealth in subsequent generations? The retired founder is grappling with a new role within the family and everyone will be affected, positively or negatively, depending on how well he accomplishes the transition. Preserving the family narrative is one worthy new role for the founder.

- *Redefining the role:* The founder must exit his business with a plan for what he will do next. Without this critical element, the founder may try to micromanage certain areas of the business, causing chaos among the employees. Furthermore, the founder often feels cast aside if he's not engaged in a plan.

- *Remembering other family members:* Everyone is affected by the sale of the business. The founder's new role will affect the entire family, and the children who had expectations of working in the business may have to find new opportunities for themselves.

- *Keeping the past alive:* The family's task is to chronicle its business history once it is no longer in the family. A fulfilling role for founders is to aid in preserving the family roots, although sometimes members of later generations will assume that task.

Chapter 3: As the family grows, the original fortune is not enough to support everyone. How can I support and encourage future wealth generators to add to the family coffers? Once again, an excellent new role for the founder is that of mentor to the next generation of entrepreneurs, but with the whole family signing off on any new venture.

- *Depleting the fortune:* Simple math tells the "rags to riches to rags in three generations" story. Without replenishing a family's wealth, it's easy to see that it can rapidly be spent in one or two generations, even without factoring in taxes and inflation. It's a matter of supporting an expanding family from a single pot of money.

- *Professionalizing the process:* Venture capital committees help families maintain a business atmosphere. When families decide to support other ventures, a committee that involves family members in the decisions will keep the process professional.

- *Mentoring the next generation:* The founder can offer invaluable guidance to rising entrepreneurs. Not everything is learned in business school. Having a seasoned wealth generator in the family is a boon to up-and-coming entrepreneurs. However, the best role is not that of a coach, but a mentor—and there is a difference.

Chapter 4: *I want the wealth to enhance our dreams, but don't want it to be the only reason we stay together.* Members of the second generation are trying to integrate the wealth into their lives and to find ways to govern themselves and the family business.

- *Meeting face-to-face:* Family meetings can take different forms depending on a family's needs. Some meetings occur at home in order to inculcate family values while the children are young. When families have complicated or explosive situations, an outside consultant may be needed to provide insight and advice that all family members will heed. A family council, established while the family owned the company, has a role even after that business has been sold.

- *Guiding the family:* The mission statement solidifies the family's core values and requires everyone's buy-in. The mission statement doesn't have to be long and complex, but one that will serve as a guiding principle for the family in times of uncertainty.

- *Governing through problems:* Governance procedures can help the family through three common family crises: staying together following the death of the founder, dealing with unproductive family members, and property management issues stemming from the sheer number of owners.

- *Preparing the next generation:* Mentoring is most effective when it involves the efforts of the entire family. As a family grows, so does its intellectual capital. Everyone has a role to play in guiding the rising generation so that its members become effective stewards of the family wealth while also pursuing individual goals.

Chapter 5: As new members come into the clan through marriage, how do I level the playing field if one partner is less wealthy, and what value do certain structures like prenuptial agreements offer me? A new member of the family can be threatening in any situation, but for families with wealth, there are often whispers of "gold digging." Families can remain unified by applying the lessons learned in dealing with the previous dilemma.

- *Understanding emotions concerning money:* Gender differences play an important role in the attitude toward wealth. Age-old truisms must be overcome in order for couples to get to the root of their differences and to articulate their philosophies—as a couple and as individuals—about money. Only then can they begin to look at structures that will put both parties at ease.
- *Easing discomfort:* Various methods help partners level the playing field with regard to the estate and their relationship to it. A variety of techniques is available for couples to explore. The important point is that they have first figured out the role that wealth plays in their lives. Only then will the techniques succeed.
- *Considering a contract:* Prenuptial agreements are among the most popular and effective solutions for many couples. This ancient and enduring custom has provided couples with written documentation of the division of their wealth. When done right, prenuptial agreements also give couples the opportunity to identify their expectations for each other—for example, who will leave the workplace to raise the children and how various financial structures will benefit the spouse and the children.

Chapter 6: I need to prepare my children and grandchildren for the responsibility of wealth, but I'm afraid that if they know too much, it will destroy any initiative to earn a living. How do I communicate this concern? This major pitfall for families of wealth is easy to slip into as the wealth becomes integrated into their lives. The third and subsequent generations are far removed from the original struggle to amass the family fortune, and self-worth can be harder to come by if the younger generations do not experience the rewards of earning a paycheck.

- *Making it on my own:* Don't underestimate the value of the self-esteem that results from earning a living. Stories abound of trust-fund babies who squander their fortune simply because they don't have to work. However, many people find that work entails more than a paycheck; it builds self-esteem and a sense of accomplishment. Older generations should think long and hard before they set up trusts that pay out vast sums of money at the age of majority.
- *Talking the talk:* Parents must recognize the elephant in the room and not let conversations about money become taboo. Children may not ask questions about the money, but that doesn't mean they are unaware of the family's wealth. Parents have to prepare children for wealth by talking about it, and by recognizing that they may have to start the conversation.
- *Walking the walk:* Parents set the best example for fiscal responsibility and offer guidance for assimilating wealth into family life. When children see parents as responsible stewards of the wealth, they begin to understand what it means to live a life that is enhanced by money.

Chapter 7: I plan to be fair to my children, but if I leave them unequal amounts of money, am I setting up a future battleground? Fair isn't always equal in estate planning. To keep a family from disintegrating, care must be taken when divvying up the pot because parents' messages around money come out loud and clear.

- *Seeking equality:* Children sometimes associate inheritance with love, which makes it more difficult for parents who want to reward responsible behavior and send a message to heirs who are not living up to their potential. While parents may be reluctant to tackle this issue, they would do better to examine their philosophy about the estate and put a clear plan in place.
- *Making intentions clear:* When parents talk to their children about their philosophy concerning money, they leave no doubts

as to their intentions. Through communication, parents not only give irresponsible children a chance to step up to the plate, they also provide an excellent opportunity to reinforce their values and beliefs with the family.

- *Structuring bequests:* Parents can choose from among a variety of methods to communicate their goals for the inheritance. There are many ways to structure estates. The important point is that parents examine each option carefully to ensure that it meets their needs and values.

Chapter 8: I want to give some of my wealth back to society, but how can I do it without my children thinking I've given away their inheritance, and in a manner that will reflect our values and enhance the family legacy? Parents walk a tightrope if they haven't prepared their children for the possibility of charitable gifts. Unmet expectations on the part of the younger generation could cause a family rift if the parents haven't previously discussed both their intentions and their children's expectations.

- *Avoiding communication:* Not talking about philanthropic legacies can lead to bitterness. Missed communication is the nemesis of generational wealth. An important opportunity for education about values is lost if parents avoid communicating with their offspring.
- *Educating the next generation:* When children understand the charitable intentions, they are more likely to embrace them. This is one of the unexpected benefits of communicating with children.
- *Becoming strategic:* An approach that blends a monetary gift with personal involvement brings greater rewards to the giver. It's not just the money; it's the full commitment. Not everyone can devote time to philanthropic activities, but those who combine it with their monetary gifts will enjoy greater satisfaction. Involving children in these efforts goes a long way toward teaching them about helping others.
- *Choosing an approach:* There are many different areas and

methods for charitable giving, depending on the donor's interests. A listing of the various approaches makes it easy for families to decide if they want to pool their money with others, start a family foundation, or gift individually.

The Family Narrative

This book is organized into three parts, all relating to a multigenerational family narrative. Part I: "Transitions and Letting Go" is from the point of view of the founder. This section emphasizes trust as a critical element—that is, the founder's ability to trust his business, or the resulting wealth from the business, to the next generation. Part II: "Retaining Family Cohesiveness" deals with the point of view of the second generation and is about discovering the family's core values, a necessary step for learning how to integrate wealth into the family. Part III: "Preparing Heirs" is from the point of view of inheritors and explores the fiscal education and psychological preparation of the heirs and their need to find self-worth beyond the money.

Because they intertwine, each section offers value for all the generations. In Part I, for example, inheritors who are distant from the founder will come to understand what their grandparents or great-grandparents achieved through their life's work and the vision these forebears had for the family legacy. Likewise, in Part III, founders will glimpse the future dilemmas of their legacy in later generations.

By using the narrative approach, we can explore the vortex of emotions that each generation brings to the eight dilemmas, and how the actions and decisions made by one generation have ramifications for those before and after. Consequently, the book contains pieces of family narratives as illustrations of these dilemmas, supplemented by advice from a cadre of experts on how to solve them.

Because the success of a family is tied to its ability to solve the dilemmas that occur in each generation, it helps to have insight into the perception of founders, inheritors, and those in the middle—the people who are closely tied to the founder, but who are also raising a generation of inheritors. Let's examine the family narrative in further detail.

All families of wealth have "how we became rich" stories, scraps of which make their way down through the generations and become legendary in the retelling of what Grandma and Grandpa sacrificed to kick-start the family fortunes. Because multigenerational wealth typically is born of a family business, the narrative begins with the founder. Once the dynasty secures its reign, issues arise with each subsequent generation. In other words, each new generation faces certain dilemmas regarding the family's accumulated wealth. From the modest beginnings of the first generation, the next one straddles a divide that is only just beginning to show its cracks. Having seen the ups and downs of the first generation's efforts, the next generation often struggles with the desire to enhance the legacy at the same time that Generation One is wrestling with how to let go.

After stamping the family with the imprimatur of wealth, the family founder wants to be able to trust the next generation to fulfill the legacy and provide stewardship for the family fortune. The identity, and often the wealth, of Generation One is still tied to the business. The trouble is, the torchbearers in Generation Two will likely have a different idea of how to expand the empire. Tensions simmer and begin to erupt. Generation Two craves both attention from the founder and independence from the family. Often, being at the same energetic stage as the founder when he started the business, Generation Two has little tolerance for acting within the structure of "the way things have always been done." In addition, members of Generation Two must learn to work together as a unit that includes siblings and sometimes cousins. The patriarch and matriarch are often still involved, as is a rising third generation that begs for coaching and mentoring.

As more generations come into the narrative, the family's link to the creator of the wealth dims, unless Generations One and Two keep it alive. Generations Three and beyond often have little connection with the founder, and view the wealth that sustains the family in an entirely different light than the first two generations.

Leslie Mayer, PhD, business psychologist and CEO of Mayer Leadership Group in Wayne, Pennsylvania, describes the psychological motives of each generation. She refers to the founder of the family fortune as the patriarch, because historically that has been more typical. "By definition, Generation One tends to be a bootstrapper," she explains. Their lack of presence at home is tolerated because the entire family is oriented around their tireless hours to create something for the family. "The associations around the founder become almost mythic." The rest of the family is often told—explicitly or implicitly—not to burden the founder with issues at home, because it is understood that "he is giving birth someplace else—to the business. This becomes the fabric of the family," Mayer says. "Everyone is sacrificing in some way, and for the children that means that anytime Dad can appear in some way it's a gift, not an expectation."

An important element of how Generation Two interacts with Generation One revolves around the mother's reaction to the gestation of the family enterprise. If she is supportive, then the children are more likely to embrace the business and hold the patriarch in high regard. If the mother harbors resentment, however, then the next generation might turn its back on the business or if they do join in, they may carry over the attitude of resentment. Of course, this is not the only reason that Generation Two might shun the family business, Mayer adds. There simply may be a desire to do something else or encouragement from Generation One to pursue a different path. If, however, there has been an unhealthy marriage in the first generation, there is significant danger that the children will inherit the tensions and "Generation Two plays out things that should have been resolved between the parents." If the mother feels victimized by the founder's devotion to the business, then the children are likely to echo the sentiment.

For Generation Two, having been raised with a mythologized father, part of the draw of entering the family business may be to curry favor and forge a bond with the patriarch. "Sometimes the business becomes a relationship connector as opposed to a child being driven to be in the business," Mayer says. Generation Two grew up with the business as part of the family, akin to a sibling, and a natural way to spend time with the founder is to relate to the business with the same passion.

Rebellion against the family company will depend on how well the children were indoctrinated into the business. Mayer points out, however, that more often than not, Generation Two feels compelled to carry on the legacy. "Overall, I tend to see more attachment than not—more 'shoulds' and 'oughts' with Generation Two."

The further a family is removed from direct and frequent interaction with the founder, the more pressing is the need to create connections. Members of Generation Three, if they are interested in entering the family business at all, are not driven to do things the way the founder intended. "They're much more challenging of the business process," says Mayer. "They didn't watch the sacrifices, and they can also feel irritated by their parents living up to ghosts." Those ghosts, Mayer says, are implicit or spoken promises made by Generation Two to Generation One. Examples of this are when siblings from Generation One have been included in the business, but prove to be unproductive. Generation Three cannot understand why Generation Two hasn't fired those siblings they consider unproductive or past their usefulness. "They see their father making adjustments because of the siblings—taking care of a ne'er-do-well, for instance. That creates a lot of tension, because Generation Two is stuck between the artifacts of Generation One and the demands of Generation Three."

Mayer supposes that if a family business still exists in the fourth and fifth generations, "a refreshed narrative gets written." There is an opportunity with this group to use its wealth freely to follow a path away from the constraints of the family business founder. The ties to the legend created generations ago tend to be tenuous, unless the founder or a leader in Generation Two has devoted time and energy to the preservation of the legacy. This is often done through such enterprises as a philanthropic foundation, a book or video, or a collection of stories and photographs.

In his film, *Born Rich,* Jamie Johnson, fourth generation heir to the Johnson & Johnson pharmaceutical fortune, notes that he has no connection to the company that bears his family name. In fact, he has to buy his Band-Aids at a drugstore like everyone else. Alternatively, the fourth generation, if it stays in the family business, can bring renewed energy and direction, as in the case of Henry Ford's great-grandson, William Clay Ford, who took over the helm of Ford Motor Company in 2001. Often, though, the family name alone is enough to cause skepticism among shareholders and employees in the company—creating a larger obstacle for potential leaders to overcome. If the family company is high profile and well-known, then family members working in the company face added pressure of living up to, or overcoming, the legend.

The importance of understanding the generational interplay in the family narrative is that the very reason wealth is accumulated is so that the founder can pass along his bounty to enrich his progeny. However, as we'll see over and over, those same generational forces, and the failure to plan for potential problems, will fracture a family and its fortunes. Take, for instance, an archetypal story of American ingenuity and wealth creation that ended with the desecration of a fortune and a family that is slowly beginning to recover—that of George Huntington Hartford's family. Told as a family narrative, the story mixes the struggle with the generational dilemmas and the emotional forces described in this book. The result is the classic "rags to riches to rags" tale for the Hartfords.

With a flair for marketing that made his retail business ubiquitous, George Huntington Hartford, a native of Maine, founded the Great Atlantic & Pacific Tea Company. He and a partner, George Gilman, opened the first store in 1859 on Vesey Street in Lower Manhattan. With the characteristic zeal of entrepreneurs, George Hartford expanded his single shop into what became the A&P grocery store chain. Two of his sons continued the vision after his death, creating a successful corporation by 1950. One son, Edward Hartford, remained on the outside, however, with no interest in the family enterprise. An immensely talented violinist, inventor, and bon vivant, he spent according to his pleasure. Withdrawing from his children, he died without passing along the work ethic his own father had embraced. A crucial family connection was lost at this point.

Edward's son, George Huntington Hartford II, grew up in a cocoon of wealth, but with the realization that his uncles were earning their way in the family business. Edward Hartford died when George Hartford II was a preteen, and George's mother continued to provide for the teenager's every wish and comfort. Determined to live a life of splendor and ease, his mother strove to heights of social grandeur. She gained a listing in the Social Register, sent her son to expensive boarding schools, hosted stunning parties at her estate in Newport, Rhode Island, and provided her son with his own chauffeur. No one appeared to be teaching the boy the value of hard work.

With a generous income from a trust fund, George Hartford II certainly had no reason to work for a living, yet he did spend some time at A&P, where his uncles insisted he prove his mettle by starting near the bottom. The Harvard graduate was relegated to the statistics department, but failed to distinguish himself as an employee and he was fired after six months. The last male heir to the company was thus cut out of the family business.

What followed was a prolonged period of womanizing, drifting, and eventually drugs. Along the way, George Hartford II attempted to become a writer, a publisher, a movie producer, a patron of the arts, and a developer. Brief spurts of success were generally followed by failure. Although not lacking in talent, George Hartford II didn't have the ambition to complete his projects.

The fourth generation proved to be both his salvation and his failure. Cathy Hartford, his daughter by his second wife, was granted a trust fund, but lacked time with her parents, which she later equated with a denial of love. She was trundled off to boarding schools and eventually descended into a world of drugs and alcohol, dying at the age of 37. By then, George Hartford was himself awash in a haze of drugs and unable to help her. When Juliet Hartford, his daughter from his third marriage, rescued him, he was elderly, ailing, and reportedly being taken advantage of by hangers-on trying to get at the last vestiges of his wealth. With the help of social service workers, Juliet Hartford moved her father from his deplorable living conditions to the Bahamas, where she happily serves as his caregiver. Today, the tremendous fortune bequeathed to George Hartford II by his industrious and creative grandfather is gone.

In the narratives of wealthy families in each section of the book, readers will see the striking similarities to their own situations, and how various solutions can prevent the breakdown of the family's financial, human, and intellectual capital. Some are well-known narratives from news accounts. Other families in this book, who shyly reveal their stories, clearly believe they are alone in what they have faced. Yet by opening up and sharing their experiences, they are contributing to the knowledge of others traveling the same road. In the cases where families wish to remain anonymous, they are referred to by fictitious names, and some of their family details have been changed.

Analysis and solutions to the family dilemmas are offered through advice from a group of wealth counselors who specialize in different aspects of wealth preservation. Their curriculum vitae are listed next.

ABOUT THE CONTRIBUTORS

Barbara Blouin, author and cofounder of The Inheritance Project, Nova Scotia.
www.inheritance-project.com
Barbara Blouin, author of *The Legacy of Inherited Wealth: Interviews with Heirs, Like a Second Mother: Nannies and Housekeepers in the Lives of Wealthy Children,* and five other publications, is a cofounder of The Inheritance Project. Blouin is an inheritor with a passionate interest in how other heirs deal with the challenges of inheriting wealth, especially at a young age.

After several years of interviewing scores of inheritors and hearing stories of conflicted and unfulfilled lives, she set out to find and interview heirs who had gone beyond the challenges and discovered rewarding ways to benefit others. The result of Blouin's study is her third book, *Labors of Love: The Legacy of Inherited Wealth, Book II.*

Olivia Boyce-Abel, founder of Boyce-Abel Associates, Santa Cruz, CA.
www.familylands.com
Olivia Boyce-Abel is founder of Boyce-Abel Associates, which assists families and individuals in the preservation of family harmony, as well as in effective and timely wealth transference and estate planning through the facilitation of family meetings and mediation of family issues. Family Lands Consulting, a branch of Boyce-Abel Associates, specializes in providing a unique focus on resolving family land decisions; both organizations advise nationally and internationally.

In addition to her work with families, Boyce-Abel has also published, presented, and lectured nationwide on numerous topics relating to wealth transference, estate planning, and family land issues. She has facilitated and taught workshops and seminars with such organizations and institutions as Yale University, Northern Trust's Family Financial Forum, Harris Bank, and the Institute of Private Investors.

Joan DiFuria, cofounder of Money, Meaning & Choices, Kentfield, CA.
www.mmcinstitute.com

Joan DiFuria, MFT, is cofounder of the Money, Meaning & Choices Institute. Her background includes eighteen years of international business expertise, twelve years as a licensed psychotherapist, and a decade of consulting, training, and presenting to high-net-worth families, financial institutions, philanthropic groups, and corporate leaders.

She works with families and family businesses and financial professionals on the noninvestment psychological issues that families face, such as passing wealth on to children; succession in the family business; and best practices that lead to the preservation of the family, the legacy, the family business, and the family wealth.

Arlene G. Dubin, author and partner in Sonnenschein Nath & Rosenthal LLP, New York City, NY.
www.sonnenschein.com

Arlene Dubin is a partner in the New York office of Sonnenschein Nath & Rosenthal LLP, a national law firm located in nine U.S. cities. She has practiced in the field of family law for more than fifteen years and is a member of Sonnenschein's Trusts and Estates Practice Group.

Dubin has extensive experience in the negotiation and drafting of prenuptial, postnuptial, paternity, cohabitation, and separation agreements. She is the author of *Prenups for Lovers: A Romantic Guide to Prenuptial Agreements*. Dubin is also a member of the New York Collaborative Law Group, which seeks to resolve matrimonial matters without litigation.

Ken Edelman, attorney specializing in estate planning, Boca Raton, FL.
Ken Edelman is an attorney with his own law firm, Kenneth Edelman, P.A., with offices in Boca Raton and West Palm Beach, Florida. His practice focuses primarily on estate, tax, and asset protection planning, as well as on business succession planning for individuals and families.

Edelman has experience in prenuptial and postnuptial agreements. He has twenty-five years of experience helping clients develop plans for tax savings, transfer of wealth through generations, and charitable giving. He also prepares clients for the potential disability issues, and works to protect clients' estates from abuse and mismanagement.

Prior to starting his own firm, Edelman managed the trusts and estates and tax practices for the Palm Beach County offices of Arnstein & Lehr, LLP and Broad and Cassel. He gives time to the Legal Aid of Palm Beach County and is involved with the Boca Raton Estate Planning Council and various charities.

David Gage, PhD, author, psychologist, and cofounder of BMC Associates, Arlington, VA.
www.bmcassociates.com
David Gage is a clinical psychologist, adjunct professor in American University's Kogod School of Business, and cofounder of BMC Associates, a multidisciplinary firm specializing in business- and estate-related conflict prevention and resolution. He is author of *The Partnership Charter: How to Start Out Right with Your New Business Partnership (Or Fix the One You're In)* and numerous articles on family business and family estate matters. His most recent articles are "Successor Partners: Gifting or Transferring a Business or Real Property to the Next Generation" in the *Journal of the American College of Trust and Estate Counsel,* December 2004, and *Estate Planning as a Family: A Collaborative Approach* published by the National Center for Family Philanthropy in 2005.

Joline Godfrey, MSW, author, founder and CEO of Independent Means Inc., Santa Barbara, CA.
www.independentmeans.com
Joline Godfrey is the founder and CEO of Independent Means Inc., based in Santa Barbara, California, and an expert in the field of financial education. She is the author of three books on financial education, including *Raising Financially Fit Kids.*

Formerly an executive for a Fortune 500 company, Godfrey is the subject of a Harvard Business School case. Her work has been featured on NBC's *Today* Show, *Oprah,* the *CBS Early Show,* and in the *New York Times, Wall Street Journal, International Herald Tribune, Business Week,* and *Fortune.* Since 1992, Independent Means has created and delivered financial education experiences for the nation's top private schools, financial institutions, and family offices.

Lee Hausner, PhD, author and partner in IFF Advisors, Irvine, CA.
www.iffadvisors.com
Lee Hausner served for nineteen years as the senior psychologist for the Beverly Hills Unified School District and is currently a clinical psychologist, business consultant, and family wealth adviser. She is the coauthor of a book on business succession planning, *Hats Off to You: Balancing Roles and Creating Success in Family Business Succession.* Hausner and Douglas Freeman coauthored *The Founder's Guide to Family Foundations,* published by the Council on Foundations. Author of many articles and books on the topic of wealth and family, she also wrote *Children of Paradise: Successful Parenting for Prosperous Families.*

Ken Huggins, professor at Monroe Community College, Rochester, NY.
Ken Huggins is Associate Professor of English at Monroe Community College in Rochester, NY. In addition to teaching college English, he has been a high school English teacher, a teacher educator, and a medical educator.

For more than fifty years, he enjoyed a summer home on Nantucket

Island until the family was forced to sell the property because they could no longer afford to maintain it. Out of the experiences with this summer property, his sister Judith Huggins Balfe, now deceased, conducted a study on owning, using, and passing on vacation homes. His booklet, *How to Pass It On: The Ownership and Use of Summer Houses,* is the companion publication to Balfe's book, *Passing It On: The Inheritance and Use of Summer Houses.*

James E. (Jay) Hughes Jr., author, retired estate planning attorney and consultant, Aspen, CO.
www.jamesehughes.com
Jay Hughes is the author of the newly expanded edition of *Family Wealth: Keeping It in the Family,* numerous articles on family governance and wealth preservation, and a series of reflections that can be found on his website.

He founded the law partnership of Hughes and Whitaker in New York City, specializing in the representation of private clients throughout the world. Hughes is now retired from the active practice of law. He frequently facilitates multigenerational family meetings with a special emphasis on mission statements and governance issues.

Hughes has spoken at numerous international and domestic symposia on international estate and trust planning. He is an emeritus member of the board of The Philanthropic Initiative, a counselor to the Family Office Exchange, an emeritus faculty member of the Institute for Private Investors, a retired member of the board of the Albert and Mary Lasker Foundation, and a former adviser to New Ventures in Philanthropy. He is also a member of the Circle of Friends of the Institute of Noetic Sciences, member of the Roundtable of the Hastings Institute, a member of the board of the Spiritual Paths Foundation, and a member of the board of the Rocky Mountain Institute. He also serves on the boards of various private trust companies and is an adviser to numerous investment institutions and a member of the editorial boards of various professional journals. Hughes was a partner of the law firms of Coudert Brothers and Jones, Day, Reavis and Pogue. He is a graduate of the Far Brook School, which teaches through the arts, the Pingry School, Princeton University, and the Columbia School of Law.

Dennis Jaffe, family wealth consultant based in San Francisco and executive director of the Family Enterprise Center at San Francisco State University.

www.dennisjaffe.com

Dennis Jaffe, PhD, helps families manage the personal and organizational issues that lead to the successful and fulfilling transfer of businesses, wealth, values, commitments, and legacies between generations. For thirty years, he has helped family businesses throughout the world deal with transition, create effective management teams, design family retreats, and build healthy relationships. As a professor at Saybrook Graduate School in San Francisco, he created the doctoral program in Organizational Systems.

Jaffe also serves as a board member and fellow of the Family Firm Institute and World Business Academy, and is a professional member of the NTL Institute and the Academy of Management. He is the author of *Working with the Ones You Love: Building a Successful Family Business* and *Working with Family Businesses: A Guide for Professional Advisors*, as well as numerous articles on family business.

Ivan Lansberg, PhD, senior partner of Lansberg, Gersick & Associates, New Haven, CT.

www.lgassoc.com

Ivan Lansberg grew up in an entrepreneurial family in Venezuela. After receiving BA, MA, and PhD degrees from Columbia University, he taught at the Columbia Graduate School of Business. Lansberg was a professor of organizational behavior at the Yale School of Organization and Management for seven years before becoming a consultant. He has advised complex family businesses in the United States, Canada, Asia, Europe and Latin America. He was one of the founders of the Family Firm Institute (FFI) and the first editor of its professional journal, *Family Business Review*. He authored *Succeeding Generations,* published by Harvard Business

School Press. Lansberg is a frequent speaker at family business programs organized by universities and industry groups. He is on the faculty of the Governing the Family Business Program at the Kellogg School of Management at Northwestern University.

Gerald Le Van, author, founder and family wealth mediator for the Le Van Company, Black Mountain, NC.
www.levanco.com
Gerald Le Van is founder and senior mediator of Le Van Company, which guides families through transitions in wealth and business. A consultant and speaker, Le Van is frequently quoted in the business press. He has written five books, including *The Survival Guide for Business Families, Raising Rich Kids,* and *Families, Money and Trouble,* and serves on the editorial boards of two national magazines.

Le Van is a trusts and estates lawyer and former law professor. He is a Fellow of the Family Firm Institute, a Fellow of the American College of Trust and Estate Counsel, a member of the International Academy of Estate and Trust Law, and former Trustee of the Presbyterian Church (USA) Foundation.

Leslie Mayer, PhD, president and CEO of Mayer Leadership Group, Wayne, PA.
www.mayerleadership.com
Leslie Mayer created Mayer Leadership Group to provide comprehensive counsel and support to CEOs and senior management teams of both growing companies and established enterprises. She coaches CEOs to improve in specific ways, such as enhancing effectiveness with the board of directors, identifying and fostering talent within the organization, creating cultures that support business objectives, managing uncertainty and the transfer of knowledge, and enhancing relationships with outside clients and partners.

Mayer is currently a senior fellow in the Management Department of the Wharton School at the University of Pennsylvania, working with the Wharton Global Family Alliance. She has been a featured speaker at various regional conferences and has been quoted in numerous publications. She currently serves on the Key Executive Services Advisory Board of Right Management Consultants, the board of directors of City Year Philadelphia, the board of directors of Point 5 Technologies, and the advisory board of the Philadelphia Writing Project. She is also a member of the Trustees' Council of Penn Women, Forum of Executive Women, Society for Psychologists in Management, and the American Psychological Association.

Jackie Merrill, founder and president of CenterPoint, Aspen, CO.
Jackiemerrill@compuserv.com

Jackie Merrill, a former Chicago executive and trained facilitator, founded CenterPoint in Aspen in 1990. The program offers four-day leadership retreats for women and couples. One core focus is on the challenges of fiscal inequality in romantic relationships. Other aspects of the program include financial management skills for women, the development of personal mission statements, managing transitions, and issues around inherited wealth.

Merrill has been a featured speaker at meetings of the Young Presidents' Organization (YPO), Avalon Trust Company in Santa Fe, Capital Guardian Trust Company, the Council on Foundations, and at other intergenerational family gatherings on the topic of fiscal inequality. She coauthored an article in *The Chase Journal* (2000), and was interviewed for the July 2004 issue of *Worth* magazine.

Merrill is also a trained storyteller and member of the National Board of Spellbinders, a volunteer organization founded as an intergenerational program to bring elders into the public schools as storytellers. She tells stories on the theme of heroes and heroines in the Aspen Valley's elementary schools.

Jessie O'Neill, MA, author and wealth counselor, Milwaukee, WI.
www.affluenza.com

Jessie O'Neill was born into wealth. She is the granddaughter of Charles Erwin Wilson, past president of General Motors and secretary of defense under President Dwight D. Eisenhower.

O'Neill is founder and director of the Affluenza Project, president of the Affluenza Healing and Education Foundation, Inc., and a licensed therapist. In her therapeutic work, O'Neill specializes in the psychology of money and wealth and how it affects both our personal and professional "bottom line" or productivity, and the treatment of "affluenza," described as a dysfunctional relationship with wealth, through a variety of educational and therapeutic services. She is the author of *The Golden Ghetto: The Psychology of Affluenza.*

Henry (Hap) Perry, founder and chairman of Asset Management Advisors, Palm Beach, FL.
www.amaglobal.com
After graduating from the Wharton School in 1970, Henry (Hap) Perry went to work for his family's businesses. He took on a variety of operational roles, leading start-up and turnaround situations in industries ranging from modular housing to undersea engineering and cable television. In addition to managing the family enterprises, he started a number of businesses on his own in the cable television, automobile, medical, and real estate fields.

Perry was inspired to found Asset Management Advisors, in 1989, by his belief in a more comprehensive approach to investing and multigenerational wealth management than could be obtained from generally accepted investment and trust companies. The firm's philosophy is built around the belief that more than money matters. The firm and its subsidiaries become long-term partners helping families address interrelated financial and human issues in order to extend their legacy into the future.

Vic Preisser, author and wealth consultant, Stockton, CA.
www.thewilliamsgroup.org
Vic Preisser brings thirty-five years' experience in business, government, and education to his partnership with Roy Williams and the Williams Group. He was formerly director of the Institute for Family Business at the University of The Pacific and the university's resident professor of management. Preisser has also served as secretary of social services and secretary of transportation for the

state of Iowa and has worked for the White House. He is a successful entrepreneur and has served in senior executive capacities with Fortune 500 companies. He received his MBA from Stanford University.

With colleague and coauthor Roy Williams, Preisser has published numerous books, including *Preparing Heirs: Five Steps to a Successful Transition of Family Wealth and Values,* and *For Love & Money: A Comprehensive Guide to the Successful Generational Transfer of Wealth.*

Ellen Remmer, vice president of TPI (The Philanthropic Initiative, Inc.), Boston, MA.

www.tpi.org

Ellen Remmer is a vice president of the Philanthropic Initiative, Inc. Since 1992, she has worked with donor clients, such as families, independent foundations, and corporations, to create strategic giving programs and practical governance structures, and with community foundations and financial services firms to strengthen their capacity to help private donors realize their philanthropic goals. She developed many of TPI's signature donor learning programs and is a frequent speaker and workshop leader on the subjects of family philanthropy, strategic giving, and women as donors.

Remmer also serves as a board member of her family's foundation, which supports programs that help disadvantaged girls take charge of their lives, and as a board member of her family's investment company. She is on the board of governors of Indiana University's Center on Philanthropy, the steering committee of Boston Funders Supporting Women and Girls, and a member of Associated Grantmakers' Program Committee.

Lisa Schneider, shareholder in the Private Wealth Services Group of Gunster, Yoakley & Stewart, P.A., West Palm Beach, FL.

www.gunster.com

A shareholder in Gunster Yoakley's Private Wealth Services Group,

Lisa Schneider concentrates her practice in estate and trust planning for high-net-worth individuals. She advises clients on their personal and business needs, including business succession planning, marital planning, the transfer of wealth from one generation to another, and tax reduction strategies involving the gifting or sale of business interests, planning for generation-skipping, and planning for charitable giving.

Schneider, a Florida board-certified trusts and estates attorney, is also admitted to practice in New York and New Jersey. She has been named one of "Best of the Bar" in the *South Florida Business Journal* and one of the Florida Legal Elite in *Florida Trend* magazine.

Roy Williams, author and wealth consultant, Stockton, CA.
www.thewilliamsgroup.org
Roy Williams has spent nearly forty years coaching successful families throughout the world. His research on 3,250 wealth-transitioning families is a logical continuation of his contributions as a trustee for Alliant University. He is an authority in the field of family coaching and frequently speaks about his research before professional groups across the nation.

With coauthor and colleague Vic Preisser, Williams has published numerous books, including *Preparing Heirs: Five Steps to a Successful Transition of Family Wealth and Values,* and *For Love & Money: A Comprehensive Guide to the Successful Generational Transfer of Wealth.*

Thayer Willis, LCSW, author and wealth consultant, Lake Oswego, OR.
www.thayerwillis.com
Thayer Willis is the author of *Navigating the Dark Side of Wealth: A Life Guide for Inheritors,* and an expert in the area of wealth counseling. Since 1990, she has specialized in helping people of all ages handle the psychological challenges of wealth.

Born into the founding family of the multibillion-dollar Georgia-Pacific Corporation, she has an insider's perspective on the privileges and tragedies that wealthy families deal with on a regular basis. She is a licensed clinical social worker. She helps people create pathways between generations, prioritize parenting tasks, and instill financial responsibility in young family members. Her programs are customized for families, attorneys, and financial professionals.

PART I

Transitions and Letting Go

FROM THE PERSPECTIVE of the wealthy family, the narrative begins with the founder of the fortune. Often the wealth springs from humble beginnings. The modest business and the tremendous vision of the founder result in the dogged pursuit of a life that is materially richer than that of his own ancestors. With a tunnel vision focused on building a business that will provide the family with financial capital, the founder may not realize the importance of preparing family members to face the unique dilemmas that will come with wealth.

As a team working together, the family can successfully cultivate all of its capital—financial, human, and intellectual—providing an edge for preserving the wealth and permitting the family legacy to take hold. If the founder sticks to the narrow vision that his children will succeed him in running the business he created, and do it the same way he did, his chances of success diminish even before the narrative takes hold.

As we'll learn in Chapter 1, businesses need to change in order to survive, and it is incumbent on the founder to let change happen. When the founder allows the family to grow by permitting each generation to pursue its own goals, the result, ironically, is a more cohesive unit. Families understand that they have many talents and that there are several paths to a rich life. While it may be difficult for the founder to let change happen, it is possible.

John D. Rockefeller, America's first recorded billionaire, sought to build a philanthropic heritage, and his legacy has continued for five generations. Business succession in Standard Oil was not forced on his son, John Jr. Instead, the younger Rockefeller carried out another part of the patriarch's vision—his deeply held beliefs in charitable giving. When John Sr. established the Rockefeller Foundation in 1913, with an endowment of $180 million, his son became its first president and one of the nation's leading philanthropists.

Today, the Rockefeller name is more widely associated with the foundation than it is with the original company. Does that mean the founder's succession plan failed? On the contrary, by remaining open to the passions of his children, and committing himself to the legacy he wanted for his family, as well as seeding the vision with start-up funds, Rockefeller was masterful in writing a lasting mission for the family narrative.

Granted, the business, regulatory, and governmental environments were different in the rough-and-tumble America of the turn of the twentieth century, but the lessons of the Rockefeller legacy are that there are many paths to succession, and the business can be the jumping-off point for enlightened families to pursue their visions in other areas. Later, in Part II, we'll discuss how various families have crafted their vision and mission.

If our family's narrative begins with the founder creating wealth through a family business, then his actions with regard to the business transition set the tone for multigenerational success. We begin in Chapter 1 with the first steps for the founder to consider; that is, to step away from leading the family's enterprise if the next generation is to take it over. In Chapter 2 we take the roles of the founder and the family a step further. When the business is sold, the family must forge a new identity, one that usually includes the management of the wealth from the sale and the continuation of the family narrative. Finally, Chapter 3 considers the next generation of entrepreneurs and how the founder can be invaluable as mentor, while the entire family fortune benefits from an infusion of capital.

Chapter One

Succession and Letting Go of a Business

THE DILEMMA:

It's time to plan for succession, but I don't know how to let go of the business.

TRANSITION IS NEVER EASY. Although the results may be rewarding later on, the effort for a business founder to present his life's work to the next generation is not exactly like turning over the car keys to a 16-year-old with a brand-new driver's license. Rather, it probably feels a little more like surrendering his newborn to a 10-year-old to raise.

Succession is surrounded by emotions that touch every part of the founder's and the family's existence. The founder may still have his wealth tied to the business and is dependent on the next generation to serve as caretaker of his financial future. Searching for a new raison d'etre, while at the same time leaving the only role he's ever known, creates tension that the entire family will experience. The next generation wants to make a change, but fears the founder's reaction. With all the issues at hand, a lack of trust fuels the fires of destruction for both the family and the business. The founder's dilemma is that he has created wealth that will support many generations of the family, but to further the business and the family, he has to find a way to allow the next generation to take over.

For a founder to overcome his reluctance to let go, he must first recognize what is preventing him from turning over the keys. The subtle unrecognized ways in which a founder displays a lack of trust in the next generation often include making vague promises for succession but with no clear process or timeline for it to occur, or by keeping the choice of successor as his and his alone, and then becoming paralyzed with indecision. Only when the founder recognizes his lack of trust in the second generation can he begin to look for ways to overcome it.

Once the successor has been named, the next generation can get down to the work of designing a process, which more than likely involves a partnership. For example, siblings may run the business together, with one of them as leader, or sometimes some of the siblings will not be involved in day-to-day operation of the company but will retain voting rights on the board of directors.

As a company matures, there may come a time when the family sells it (how this affects the founder and the family will be examined in Chapter 2). In this scenario, the wealth from the sale becomes the new "family business." In another example, the family relinquishes some or all of its control by going public. The succession issue in this situation may include a leader from the outside, changing the family dynamic with respect to the business. In this chapter, we'll examine many of the elements involved in succession, which become all the more complex when tangled with family issues. We will discuss the following major topics: failing to transition, choosing a successor, aiding the succession, and going public.

Failing to Transition

Most businesses don't make a successful changeover from one generation to the next. With some 80 percent of businesses in North America and 75 percent in the United Kingdom classified as family businesses according to the Family Firm Institute, succession planning is crucial for families seeking to pass on the company they have spent a life building. If the business fails between the first and second generations, the family likely will lose its wealth. To add insult to injury, a family rift could result if the transition is handled poorly.

Whether they own Fortune 500 family-controlled businesses like Wal-Mart, or Mom-and-Pop stores, families that don't plan to eventually sell the business must resolve succession issues, usually involving the next generation of children or nieces and nephews. Many people do not know how to plan so that both the family and the business remain intact.

"Because of the distortion and bias that comes with nepotism, it's really common for smart people to make stupid judgments," says Ivan Lansberg, an organizational psychologist and principal at Lansberg, Gersick & Associates. Succession issues in a family business are among the most difficult, and the reasons are varied. Often the fear of letting go drives founders to make decisions that are inconsistent with what makes sense for the business. The founder may retain control for too long, continuing to do things the old way, and thus preventing needed progress. Creating a succession plan that removes that fear will go a long way toward resolving issues of trust.

Jay Hughes, retired tax and estates attorney, author, and consultant, maintains that most succession plans fail because the first generation tries to impose its dreams on the second, setting up a cycle for dysfunction and eventual collapse. "The families that fail fast are the ones where the first generation says to the second 'you'll do this for us, and then we'll do something for you,'" he says. "It's better to ask, 'what is your dream, and how can the family enhance it?'"

John D. Rockefeller had that perspective, says Hughes, simply because he did not require his son to succeed him in his Standard Oil enterprise. On the other hand, Henry Ford's only son, Edsel Ford, was expected to take part in the family business, and ascended to the presidency at the age of 25. Although he showed a talent for the business, it was generally agreed that he was not happy, and ulcers resulted from his inner conflict. He died at the age of 49, and Hughes believes that had it not been for the business aptitude and enthusiasm of Henry Ford II, Edsel Ford's son, the Ford Motor Company would have been lost to the family in a single generation.

Dennis Jaffe, a professor at Saybrook Graduate School, maintains there are two key reasons family businesses fail to transition. The first is that the family uses the business as a means of providing jobs to family members who are unqualified or who see the business as an extension of the family budget, and thus weaken it by using funds for nonbusiness reasons. The second reason, Jaffe says, is that "the entrepreneur runs the business the way he always has," so the business isn't renewed and eventually becomes stale.

As stated earlier, there are many different reasons, some unspoken or unconscious, why a founder fails to choose a successor. Sometimes he names a successor, but doesn't follow through with a process for the transition. Chief among the worries is that the founder wants the successor to run the business as he would, yet also to continue its success. What he often doesn't realize is that those may be opposing forces—to continue the success of the business might mean that the business has to change. The first item on the founder's succession agenda should include a process and policies that help him overcome his worries and allow both him and the successor to trust each other. As we'll see, it starts with communication.

Choosing a Successor

The selection of a successor should not rest on the shoulders of the founder, as in the story of John Roberts (not his real name). Roberts, CEO of a family business in the Midwest, has given his sons no timeline for when he might leave the firm. He says he doesn't plan to retire anytime soon, but when he does, his sons are his succession plan. "I'll probably die on the job," he says.

Roberts is currently riding the wave of a business success. Since his two sons joined him in earnest in the early 1990s, his business has grown twelvefold. Both sons, now 32 and 34, have had integral roles in expanding and running the business. But the day will come when one will be anointed to lead the companies, and Roberts claims the choice of that leader will be his alone. By Roberts's description, both sons are "natural leaders and extroverts." For now the three men are directing the company as a team, with one son as president, and the other son as chief operating officer.

The first and second generations often have difficulty predicting the success or failure of succession planning because while the original players are still active and controlling the business, there is no family history of transition to draw on. Consequently both generations may be overly optimistic about the outcome and unable to anticipate the challenge that stalls succession decisions. In this situation, it is Roberts's retention of the choice of successor.

Yet Jaffe says that in any family that tries to make Roberts's "almost biblical" choice between two sons, the underlying factor is a lack of trust that may have nothing to do with the abilities of the potential successors. A "my way or the highway" approach to leading the business may prevent the founder from letting anyone run the company or it may be that the second generation hasn't yet proved its leadership ability.

Lee Hausner, PhD, partner with IFF Advisors, suggests that putting the father in charge of making such a momentous family decision is a mistake. Hausner describes a family she is working with that is experiencing a similar gut-wrenching choice. In this case, the son and the son-in-law both want to run the business. On paper, the son-in-law is more qualified, but the son spent his life working in the family business. "The father became paralyzed with having to make this decision."

Hausner advised them to allow their company's board of directors to resolve the issue based on policies previously set by the board and the family. Meanwhile she is meeting with the family and asking each of them to identify the strengths of each candidate. This process often enables family members to separately draw the same conclusion as the board.

After reviewing the operational plans of each contender, the board chose the son-in-law to lead the company. "The son is not happy, but my job is to make sure these two can work as a team now," Hausner says. When such a momentous decision has been made, families need help to maintain both family unity and the business vision.

Ivan Lansberg says that when it comes to succession, there will always be "letting go issues and taking charge issues." He adds, "What's really missing, surprisingly, is a method for letting go." When policies and procedures are in place, the founder has outlets to aid in the decision, and that decision will be clear to the family and business members.

Policies can be developed by the company's board or by the family council. A family council, discussed in greater detail in Part II, operates like an advisory board for the family and the family business. It consists of family members, and it serves different roles depending on family and business needs, as well as on the expertise of the members. Because family and business are so closely tied, it often makes sense to have the family council set the policies because these are the people who understand the nuances that exist in a family business. The family council is the first organized "board" the family should establish.

Once the company matures, some families choose to establish a formal board of directors that includes family members as well as outsiders, and which is solely focused on the business. In that case, the family council exists as a separate entity and still contributes enormous value as a bridge between business and family, taking on a variety of tasks that a board of directors might not typically focus on, such as mentoring family members, establishing philanthropic initiatives, and more, as we'll see in later chapters. With respect to the family business, the council's role is to intersect family and company. The council's tasks include keeping the entire clan informed about the company, even those not directly involved in the business; preparing family members who want to have a role in the business; and interacting with the board of directors, if there is one.

With respect to establishing a set of policies for the business, it takes time and careful thought, but both are worthwhile because the policies will continue to assist families in making decisions— especially the messy ones that go along with being both a family and a business. "All the problems in family business boil down to eight or nine issues," says Hausner. "If families develop policies they could avoid heartache and get things objectified." That would lead to more trust among family members, because they could point to the policy in times of disagreement. Hausner recommends the following policies:

- **Mission and vision for the business.** Just as in a family, the mission and vision will keep the family business on track, as discussed in Part II.

- **Method for communication.** All too often, if there is no set method and time to disseminate information, such as a monthly meeting with an agenda, communication will be on a catch-as-catch-can basis, leaving the vision, mission, and even daily operating procedures open to interpretation.

- **Procedures for hiring family (including spouses) and nonfamily.** Objective standards for hiring will prove invaluable when applicants have to be turned down. When the standards are spelled out and specific, applicants can't claim that family members were favored.

- **Compensation guidelines.** Once again, this avoids family members or nonfamily employees claiming that they were treated unfairly.

- **Performance reviews.** Family members and nonfamily personnel need to know how they are being evaluated and, in the case of nonfamily employees, if there is a path for advancement for them.

- **Training programs.** Founders shouldn't assume that because employees are family members, they have somehow "soaked up" all they need to know about the business.

- **Communication with shareholders.** Communication should include people in the family who are not working in the business. The family council is ideal for keeping everyone in the loop and information should be delivered regularly.

- **Company's role in philanthropy and community service.** Employees will be more likely to buy into the philanthropic efforts when they understand what they are, and the company's vision for a legacy.

When these policies are in place, not only will the business run more smoothly, but the founder will have objective criteria for determining a range of issues, including succession. The choice of who will lead the company will not appear to the potential successors to be made at the whim of the founder. In fact, the choice will sometimes become evident through the policies because potential successors will be clearly identified in the communication among the family members, they will have a process for training, and they will know what to expect in terms of performance and compensation.

Families tend to become lax in establishing and enforcing policies for their own business, Hausner notes, but they should operate the company as if it were run by outsiders. A company can go under when it fails to institute a policy that many would think of as a no-brainer, such as how much employees are paid, making the loss of the company all the worse because it was seemingly so easily avoidable. Because families so often personalize business issues, they may attribute the higher salary of another family member to bias on the part of the founder. Written guidelines will dispel that notion.

Hausner offers the following example. Compensation issues, specifically yearly bonuses, are bringing down a family she is counseling. One currently out-of-favor son-in-law received a fraction of the bonus other family members received, and there is no policy to outline how bonuses are determined. The angry underpaid son-in-law is planning to bring up this issue at the next board meeting, which is sure to be filled with the fireworks and resentments that Hausner forecasts could force the sale of the multimillion-dollar company.

As we travel through the narratives of this book, we'll see time and time again that effective, clear, and consistent communication is a cornerstone to building a solid family and sustaining both the family and the fortune. Therefore, it is incumbent on the first generation to ensure that all family members have a say in family matters; and a family council is an excellent venue for solidifying the family's intent.

The family in the next example spent years sorting through the fallout from miscommunication with regard to the business succession plan. No communication is often as bad as miscommunication, and when the founder's succession plan leaves room for interpretation, it is to the detriment of the next generation waiting in the wings. At the very least, it's a lost opportunity for training and mentoring. At worst, families often simmer with resentment over unmet expectations. Whether the founder has plans to sell the business or prepare his children to eventually take over, as John Roberts did, the children won't understand the decision if they haven't been kept in the loop. Miscommunication or vague promises of "taking all of this over someday" may be indications that the founder is unwilling to turn over his business to the next generation.

Jim Liautaud of Chicago, founder of several successful businesses in the Midwest, started out with a vision for succession planning within the family—the family would own the businesses, but not run them. But his second son saw things differently and thought he was going to be anointed to lead the companies.

Liautaud's son, Jimmy John Liautaud, is now a successful entrepreneur in his own right, but says that before he started his own sandwich shop empire he assumed his father had a place for him in the family business. "I didn't think about what I needed to do because he had it all figured out for us. I believed this from the time I remember."

It's on this point that his and his father's stories diverge. Jimmy John Liautaud says his father promised him a leadership position in the family business. "I was supposed to be taking over everything. I thought all this would happen before I reached 30, but I didn't even get a phone call. Where were my keys to the kingdom?"

Jim Liautaud doesn't remember promising that magic age to any of his children. He abhorred the thought of leaving operating succession to the second generation. "I never wanted my children in my business, or running my business, because they, and everyone else, would be comparing their performance to mine. Statistics prove the chances of the chosen son—or any son—of an aggressive, successful entrepreneur matching the talents of his parent are slim," he says. "I told them they could hire pros to run the businesses or sell them and use the money to invest on their own."

Jim Liautaud later changed his mind when he began to see his grown children in a different light. Two of his children had not only expressed an interest in owning and running the businesses, but had proven themselves competent leaders of other businesses. Around that same time, Liautaud was ready to make the transition. In his estate plan, most of the companies were transferred to the children. Each of the four siblings now owns an equal 25 percent of the equity. Jimmy John Liautaud, who by then had established himself as the most successful entrepreneur, was tapped to exercise a majority voting control and the oldest son became CEO. The remaining two siblings do not have positions in the business, but all four agreed on who should have roles in the company and what those roles would be. The Liautauds spent time repairing a rift over miscommunication that could have been avoided if there had been a clear process for transition that accompanied the promise. The second generation is now working well together, running the companies their father transferred.

Communication has to be clear and consistent to be effective. Otherwise hurt feelings result over unspoken assumptions. As we'll learn in Part II, founders who begin consistent communication when children are young can set expectations and head off strife later. As subsequent generations expand and are written into the narrative, the effort has to be even more focused so that no individual member feels adrift.

Lee Hausner, who helped the Liautauds through their transition, points out that different generations have different visions and the two are not always connected. Miscommunication is typical. When the first and second generations are faced with the transition of the company, "both generations have to work toward the middle," she says, "and everyone in the family has to march toward the mutual goal."

Effective communication is high on her list of the essential family-business policies because without those skills, the family will never resolve any of its challenges. "Families in business are always striving to balance three important issues: business prosperity, family harmony, and personal well-being," she says. "No one wants to have a stomachache whenever they see their brother or sister. We all want that Norman Rockwellian vision of a family praying together around the Thanksgiving turkey and family members want to have their personal dreams and passions recognized. How successfully these critical needs are accommodated will be the result of the effectiveness of the communication process."

Once communication is established, further policies on the list point to the processes that make the succession and transition issues stick. Dennis Jaffe recommends that anytime a business succession plan is discussed, a clear process should accompany the discussion. "Succession is not a prize, it's something you have to earn," he says. A well-designed path for succession will ensure the successor understands what has to be done along the way to leadership.

A family Jaffe counseled was similar to the Liautauds in that there was conversation about succession in the business when the children were young. Based on that conversation, the children made certain assumptions, but ultimately were disappointed when their father didn't follow through. "People have emotional ways of seizing on information, rather than clarifying it," says Jaffe. When families state policies concerning their business decisions up front, and ensure that every family member is clear on the process and guidelines, the opportunity for misinterpretation is diminished and families avoid distress over the founder's intentions.

Along with communication, training will be most effective when family members are taught as youngsters. The potentially ugly results of sibling rivalry can be tamped if training includes the values of collaboration and partnership.

According to Hausner, family business succession is "an endangered species" because, in many cases, the root of destruction is sibling rivalry, with "everyone trying to be Mom or Dad." If siblings can't learn collaboration, the business is doomed in one generation. In families like the Roberts, the second generation has had practice in collaboration, and can divide areas of business leadership and responsibility. Hausner advises families to instill teamwork early by teaching children to work together through support for charitable causes or by bringing them in on family business decisions as soon as they are ready.

Indeed, Roberts began working the boys in the company when they were only 10. By age 15 or 16, they were out on the road selling the company's products. "I paid them," Roberts says. "When wages were $5, I paid them $7 or $8." His father took note of the work ethic in his grandsons and tried to woo them to his own business, but Roberts outmaneuvered him. "I trumped him by upping their pay." Roberts also gave the boys some ownership responsibility at an early age. "I saw a big difference when they owned something," he says. "They owned and raised heifers, and theirs were always a little better cared for than [mine]."

Roberts's son, Mike Roberts (not his real name), now says that his father enlightened him on the opportunities in commerce early on, which meant that he and his brother saw no reason not to continue in the family business after college. "We were a small company at that time, and growing. We had a good product, and everyone could see that." As the company continues to grow, the tradition of working together as a team still holds.

Giving successors a role in the business early, or a taste of entrepreneurship, allows them to decide if the family company, or indeed, commerce at all, is going to be their path. If they choose entrepreneurship, but want to go in a different direction, there is an important role for the founder and the family, as we'll explore in Chapter 3. But by teaching collaboration and teamwork, the founder is setting the stage for a successful transition because the players will already have experience in working together. The founder will trust their ability to continue the business as a team, and not as individuals seeking dictatorship, and thus cutting off the rest of the family.

As we'll see next, the second generation has to have an operating plan in place that the founder approves. But first, both generations have to complete an assessment of the company's health in order to make the transition a success.

Aiding the Succession

The first and second generation can work together to ensure the business transitions successfully. The post-succession period is a critical juncture for family business success, because an entirely new operating model has to be instituted. Instead of a sole owner with single-minded focus, the business is now likely being led by a partnership of siblings, often with a controlling owner among them or one of them serving as CEO. Decisions can no longer be made by one person, that is the founder. Collaboration is the key to success at this stage. The founder may opt to stay involved in the business, but he mustn't hinder the plans of the next generation. If the reins have been handed over, the founder has to step aside and allow the successors to run the business, and the successor CEO (or controlling owner) has to work with the input of the other family stakeholders.

A family business assessment inventory, developed by Dennis Jaffe, is the first step in a business assessment because if the business and family are healthy, there will be fewer concerns from the founder and the successor regarding the transition. Ideally the founder will feel secure in passing along a business that is shipshape, and the successor will trust and admire the founder's abilities.

Because the family is so tied up in the business at this point, the health of the business is also an indication of the condition of the family. Jaffe's premise is that it is difficult to have a healthy business if the family is unhealthy, and vice versa. Transitioning a healthy business to an unhealthy family, or asking a family member to make a success of a family business that has become its own worst enemy, will mean failure for the transition and for the wealth. Consequently, Jaffe designed his Family Business Assessment Inventory to explore some of the key qualities for maintaining healthy businesses and families. Every family is unique, he says, but whatever a family's areas of contention are, they need to be resolved. Each of the six sections of the inventory relate to a specific aspect of the business.

Jaffe recommends that each family member take the assessment separately, and then collect scores. Although there are no right and wrong answers, the assessment will point out the most common areas where scores are low, indicating a need for the family to focus on them. Likewise, if there are widely differing scores in a particular area, the family should discuss that topic. Jaffe has a new, expanded version of the assessment, in which a professional works with the family. The version shown here can give families a quick indication of the business and family health.

The assessment is a good starting point for discussion within the family council. Armed with the results of the assessment, the council can begin discussions that may span several meetings and three generations of family—the retiring founder, the active second generation, and the up-and-coming third generation. A question that reveals a disparity among answers is a good place to begin. The family should seek to ensure that everyone understands the business, how it relates to the family and to each of them individually, and what the vision is for how the business will help all of them achieve their goals.

Although the assessment gives families an indication of areas they need to improve, for a business to succeed from one generation to the next, it has to evolve into a professionally managed company. There are sea changes that a family company goes through as it sheds its "familycentric" skin.

Jaffe points out that successful businesses go from "personality centered to business centered, and act more like a business and less like a one-man shop." The successful business will go beyond a family council and a set of essential policies established by the founder to a more formal board of directors and a method for managing process developed by the next generation, which includes more dimensions than were considered by the original founder. "Basically the family goes from being family first to being business first."

Lee Hausner describes the transition of a family business from its founding to its continued success through the next generation as if it were a slope. There is the "entrepreneurial spirit that fires the business" in the beginning and starts the upward climb. Near the top of the slope, there is a critical transition when the business has to become "professionalized." Perhaps more sophisticated technology needs to be introduced or strategic planning initiated. Basically, an infrastructure has to be built before the business can grow.

If successful, the slope of the business continues its upward direction. If not, it curves back down and the business fails. The point where the business needs to be professionalized is a very

THE FAMILY BUSINESS ASSESSMENT INVENTORY

For each question below, circle the number that most nearly describes how strongly you agree or disagree with the statement:

3 = Strongly Agree   2 = Agree Somewhat
1 = Disagree Somewhat   0 = Strongly Disagree

Scale 1: MISSION/PLANNING

1. People know what our business stands for.   3   2   1   0
2. We have a business plan that is evaluated
   and updated regularly.   3   2   1   0
3. There is a written succession plan
   for the next generation of the business.   3   2   1   0
4. As our business grows, our profit has
   risen as well.   3   2   1   0
5. We share our dreams and visions for the future,
   and know what each family member wants.   3   2   1   0

Scale 1 TOTAL (Add all circled numbers together): _____

Scale 2: COMMUNICATION/CONFLICT RESOLUTION

1. Our family meets several times a year to talk
   about how things are going.   3   2   1   0
2. There are no deep conflicts in our family that
   have caused family members to cut themselves
   off from each other.   3   2   1   0
3. Our family openly expresses differences of opinion.   3   2   1   0
4. We are able to resolve our major conflicts
   and differences.   3   2   1   0
5. We have a clear process for making different
   types of decision.   3   2   1   0

Scale 2 TOTAL (Add all circled numbers together): _____

Scale 3: BUSINESS PARTICIPATION

1. We evaluate clearly and objectively the performance of each family member in the business.   3   2   1   0
2. Women participate in the business with
   equal opportunities.   3   2   1   0
3. Family members feel they are treated fairly
   in business-related matters.   3   2   1   0

THE FAMILY BUSINESS ASSESSMENT INVENTORY
(cont'd.)

4. Family employees know where they stand in
the business, including limits and opportunities.   3   2   1   0
5. Family members in the business have
clear responsibilities and roles.   3   2   1   0

Scale 3 TOTAL (Add all circled numbers together): _____

Scale 4: OUTSIDE ADVICE

1. The head of the business doesn't have to be
involved in everything, or control everything.   3   2   1   0
2. The business is able to hire and retain
nonfamily managers in responsible positions.   3   2   1   0
3. We listen to and consider new ideas from our
younger generation and outside managers.   3   2   1   0
4. We share our planning with nonfamily managers.   3   2   1   0
5. Outside advisors meet with us regularly
and have been willing to give us "bad news."   3   2   1   0

Scale 4 TOTAL (Add all circled numbers together): _____

Scale 5: GENERATIONAL CONTINUITY

1. Offspring have been able to learn about
the business from their parents.   3   2   1   0
2. There has been some discussions and planning
for the possible roles of heirs as they enter
the business.   3   2   1   0
3. Heirs have had a chance to work elsewhere.   3   2   1   0
4. Offspring feel that plans for the division
of the business are fair.   3   2   1   0
5. Offspring have opportunity to influence
the future of the business.   3   2   1   0

Scale 5 TOTAL (Add all circled numbers together): _____

Scale 6: OUTSIDE THE BUSINESS

1. The family spends time together relaxing
in nonbusiness activities.   3   2   1   0
2. Our family is active in the community.   3   2   1   0

THE FAMILY BUSINESS ASSESSMENT INVENTORY
(cont'd.)

3. Everyone in the family is actively involved
   in fitness and in caring for his or her health.   3   2   1   0
4. Family members in the business have outside
   hobbies or interests.   3   2   1   0
5. We encourage each person in the family to
   discover his or her own way.   3   2   1   0

Scale 6 TOTAL (Add all circled numbers together): _____

Scoring and Using the Inventory

Fill in the scores of each member of the family who completes the inventory below. Then take the average of all the scores and calculate the difference between the two family members with the highest and lowest scores. Some scales may not be relevant to your family business.

	Founder	Spouse	Heir	Heir	Relative	Average	Difference Between Highest & Lowest
Name:							
Scale 1:							
Scale 2:							
Scale 3:							
Scale 4:							
Scale 5:							
Scale 6:							

Your score on each scale can be between 0 and 15. A score below 5 on any scale indicates that you perceive some difficulty in that area. Scores between 6 and 10 on a scale indicate some strain in that area. Scores over 11 indicate you perceive your family business as doing very well in that area.

(From *Working with the Ones You Love: Building a Successful Family Business* by Dennis Jaffe, pp. 42–45. Reprinted by permission.)

difficult transition for the entrepreneur, says Hausner, but it is imperative for the founder to embrace the concept and to trust the next generation. "You can't run a $100 million business like a start-up."

Why is this business transition critical? Imagine the typical scenario of a family company and how it begins: The founder has an idea for how to make money. He may go it alone or join up with a sibling or spouse. When founders form their start-ups, they are forced to be essentially one-person shows. They develop products or services, sell them, collect the money, write the checks, and lock the door at night—usually late at night. As the business grows, they typically micromanage their employees. "Many entrepreneurs' strong suit is control. It is not delegating," says David Gage, PhD, cofounder of BMC Associates.

Because founders "ran the whole show" and often continue operating that way even as they hire more employees, it is difficult for them to accept the idea that their children with business degrees can step into the company and begin delegating roles and authority to the very same employees they, the founders, had always kept on very short leashes.

According to Gage, a founder may experience anxiety as his children talk about expanding into new markets and new lines of business, which is understandable because he believes the business worked just fine the way he ran it. "While the next generation may be chomping at the bit to make change, the founder may still be reluctant to allocate company profits toward a way of conducting business that he doesn't understand. Businesses usually fail at this juncture if the founder can't step away."

Gage adds that a partnership plan will help the next generation define the governance of the business. For example, the four second-generation Liautaud siblings—some actively involved in the business and some not—were able to come to agreement about how to run the company their father transferred to them, in large part because they applied business principles to the process. Because the next generation will become a team of partners, Gage recommends that they develop a partnership charter, ideally before they take over the management from their parents, and before they become co-owners.

The benefit of the charter, Gage points out, is that it is a way to document the next generation's discussions, negotiations, and agreements on a range of business and interpersonal issues. It differs from partnership or shareholder agreements, which are legal documents. A charter is not legally binding, but is frequently used to clarify and set the terms of future corporate documents. Some of the reasons for partners, or future partners, to create a charter are as follows:

- To provide a structure in which to discuss sensitive and difficult issues.
- To remove the ambiguity that exists in many partner relationships.
- To help partners reach written agreements about their personal styles and values and their expectations for one another, as well as business details.
- To memorialize their negotiations and agreements.
- To serve as a guide for working and owning together for years to come.
- To greatly diminish the likelihood of misunderstandings and conflicts.

One of the major business issues for next-generation family members to work out—besides compensation and ownership—is the who-will-do-what question, Gage notes. The potential roles for siblings working together are extremely diverse—from running the business to being a "silent" investor with a seat on the board of directors. If they, as adults, are given the opportunity to work out their roles and their partnership themselves, they will be more invested in the outcome, and will have a better chance of feeling good about their arrangement—much better, Gage maintains, than if a parent selected those roles for them.

Gage developed his philosophy regarding the necessity of sibling partners to determine their own fate from his years mediating disputes among siblings who had their business arrangements determined by their parents. "Adult children in their 30s, 40s, and 50s do not want their parents determining the nature of their relationships with their brothers and sisters. Children develop a wisdom about their sibling relationships that parents have to put their trust in," he says.

Gage has seen many instances in which a parent's desire for his children to work together was not matched by the children's ability to function as a team. "It's truly sad in some cases because the siblings had perfectly fine relationships before the parents invited an additional sibling into the business, or before gifting stock to all the children, effectively locking them in as business partners." Sometimes, he says, the arrangement parents devise for their children is workable. Yet allowing them to figure it out for themselves makes all the difference in terms of the long-term success of the future partners. The process of discussing, negotiating, and drafting written agreements is as important as the final document.

After siblings create a charter that spells out in detail how they would propose to co-own and operate the family business together, and if the parents believe the plans are unworkable, they have the right and responsibility to communicate this to the children and not transfer the business to them. Gage believes this is a reasonable and businesslike stance to take, especially in situations where children will buy out parents over time and the success of the buyout (and often the parents' retirement) hinges on the ability of the siblings to work together. "Parents maintain thumbs-up or thumbs-down control over their children, which is much more respectful than meddling in their arrangement with one another."

Gage maintains that he has never seen parents reject a partnership charter that adult children have proposed to their parents, however. "The level of planning that must occur for people to complete a partnership charter is so detailed and intense that children develop a high level of confidence in themselves, which builds their parents' confidence in them as well."

He offers a sample of how a partnership charter could be structured. It begins with a preamble, which states the broad goals of the individuals who are becoming partners. The first section of the charter will include such business issues as vision and strategic direction, ownership, titles, roles, management of the employment guidelines, and compensation. The second section concerns the relationship among the partners, and includes personal styles and how to work together, personal and corporate values, and expectations of the partners. The third section is about the future of the business and the partners, and includes creating guidelines for unexpected events, resolving disputes, and effective communication.

The importance of siblings having some sort of governance system that recognizes that they are distinct from the founder, and that they are working as a team, is vital for the business to transition successfully. Otherwise, the business struggles or breaks up over the inability of the family to come to terms.

For the descendents of one of America's pioneering wine growers, the inability to develop a partnership created a family schism that lasted nearly half a century. Not only could the Mondavi brothers not work together or respect each other, but they also passed their disputatious ways on to the next generation. Scions of the famous Charles Krug winery founded by their father, the two siblings, Robert and Peter Mondavi, argued regularly and vehemently about every aspect of the business. After allegedly punching Peter Mondavi during an altercation, Robert Mondavi was put on paid leave. He left the family company in 1965 and formed the Robert Mondavi Corporation, which he planned to leave to his own two sons. On paper, the lack of collaboration between the two brothers would seem to have led to two separate, successful family businesses. But the story doesn't end here.

Perhaps hampered by his own inability to get along with his brother, Robert Mondavi failed to encourage or instill a devotion to the business and teamwork in his own potential successors. He forced his sons to work together despite their disparate natures. The two sons carried out the belligerent family narrative, paralyzing the firm. Ultimately, one son, Timothy Mondavi, took a sabbatical and moved to Hawaii. Robert Mondavi later helped to oust his other son, who had been serving as chairman.

Robert Mondavi's admittedly controlling streak wasn't strong enough to force collaboration among his successors. The company went public in 1993, and Mondavi is said to be mending relations with his sons. In his book, *Harvests of Joy,* Mondavi writes, "Out of all the rigidities and mistakes of my past, I've learned one final lesson, and I'd like to see it engraved on the desk of every business leader, teacher, and parent in America: The greatest leaders don't rule. They inspire."

The story has a final chapter, perhaps written to inspire the next generation. Now in their 90s, and more than forty years after their altercation, Peter and Robert Mondavi and their sons are attempting a collaboration. The family planned to produce a barrel of wine and bottle sixty magnums to sell at the annual Napa Valley Auction. Although it's an admirable show of unity, the gesture might be "too little, too late" to continue the Mondavi company family tradition. Peter Mondavi's sons are still in business together at Charles Krug, but Robert Mondavi's sons have no part in the Mondavi business, thus ending the family reign in only the second generation.

There is a twist to the challenge of collaboration in the next generation. What if the next generation is governing effectively, but the founder is the hindrance? There are many ways for founders to meddle, effectively stalling business transition and growth. Even in families where the next generation is operating smoothly, many have tales of a reluctant founder who is slowly receding from business management, but still unable to cut the last remaining strings. They are the ones who travel for months at a time, only to swoop in periodically to micromanage and cause chaos within the business and angst among successors, who have been managing the company day in and day out. Founders can stay involved in the business, but once the reins of succession have been passed, they need to let the next generation take over. By micromanaging in specific areas of the business, founders often don't realize the disorder they generate among the employees and new management.

Errant founders "can be managed," says Ivan Lansberg, "but it depends on the particular cast of characters, and the degree to which there are options for involvement that are real and defined. Controlling owners are often monarchic in terms of retirement style," he adds, and understanding the particular style of the entrepreneur is critical. He points out that founders who act like monarchs or generals, maintaining "my way or the highway" approaches to management, are the most difficult to phase out. "There are not many answers, other than waiting them out or walling them into a specific area of the company."

When Lansberg works with families trying to handle this situation, he approaches it from four intervention levels:

1) Work with the entrepreneurs to "think through their unrealized ambitions that can be channeled in different ways, for example philanthropy or politics. Some become university presidents, or researchers, if they have an engineering bent." Lansberg says that when asked to dig deep, entrepreneurs usually find other areas that interest them besides managing a business.

2) Determine the governance structures that allow the entrepreneur to be productive and to provide the wisdom that comes from starting the business from the ground up, yet not impact the day-to-day routines. It could mean leading a board of directors or establishing a family foundation. Lansberg says, "Suddenly, they have a whole slew of tasks they can do and they feel productive."

3) Work within the social context of the players, so founders assume the role of encouraging ongoing development of the successor and they feel comfortable passing the baton.

4) Plan the transition process. "It's really getting people to agree on timing," according to Lansberg. When he works with clients, he draws a horizontal line on a piece of paper, and writes the word "today" at the far left side. "I give it to the controlling owner and ask him to write a date when he will be out of management totally, and then we determine what specifically needs to happen to get there. The moment they begin to conceptualize what it takes to bring about the transition, it becomes real rather than an amorphous leap of faith." According to Lansberg, all four levels of intervention are required. "Multiple leverage points work. If you just do one, you're likely to fail."

Going Public

Sometimes the family must relinquish its full control and move to outside leadership. When this happens, the family faces a somewhat different challenge. Outsiders now become part of the narrative of the company, and everyone must learn to work under more professional strictures.

As family businesses grow and mature, they sometimes don't stay in the family, and that may be the best option for a variety of reasons. Perhaps the company becomes too large and unwieldy for the family to control or perhaps too many family members want to take their proceeds from the business and go in separate directions. Competition may have become too great or the nature of the business may have changed. With foresight, families can take advantage of good timing, but they have to realize that the dynamic of the family business will shift even more to a professional and impersonal enterprise.

Taking their family business public was the right decision for the Hughes family of Orlando, Florida. Money from the sale of the business provided the means to grow a small local company into a multistate conglomerate. According to David Hughes, current chairman of the company, relinquishing control was not difficult for him, perhaps because the decision to sell stock to the public had been made a generation ago. Once the company was on that path, family control steadily declined with the continued sale of shares.

The family narrative begins with David's grandfather, Clarence Hughes, who moved from Indiana to Florida in 1920. There he began a modest electrical contracting business, which he called Hughes and Sons. "They wired houses and commercial buildings," says Hughes.

At the age of 27, Clarence's son Russell Hughes decided that he was "sick and tired of the wiring business and wanted to go into the supply side." Hughes Electrical Supply, now called Hughes Supply, was born. Today the company is a wholesale distributor of a vast array of construction products, with branches in thirty-eight states.

Because it was Clarence's sons who expanded the business into what it is today, David Hughes counts himself as second generation rather than third to run the family enterprise. As is typical in families who develop a commercial enterprise, David Hughes was encouraged to pursue a professional career, and earned a law degree. But the lure of the family business proved too great and, in 1967, he joined as assistant dispatcher, "a fancy name for a truck loader," he jokes. "I came close to working for General Electric, but I realized this was the way to go. My Uncle Russell pretty much insisted his son work for the business, but my brother and I had more flexibility."

Coming in as he did, near the bottom of the business hierarchy, and moving his way up is one of the two most effective portals into the family business, Hughes believes. The other way is to work outside the family business to gain expertise and then, after a certain number of years, to come into the fold. Either scenario provides the family member with some credibility. Experts agree that the increased scrutiny for successors within the family can be a blessing and a curse for family businesses, especially if they've gone public and are now answerable to outside shareholders.

The transition to a public company began in 1970, as Russell and Clarence Hughes were beginning to face their mortality. With the bulk of their wealth tied to the family business, they were fearful they would die without enough money to pay estate taxes. They raised funds by selling a minority portion of their stock, and put the money in municipal bonds so it would be a ready source of cash.

Lansberg says that unlike the Hughes family, which based its decision to go public on the personal estate-planning decisions of David Hughes's uncle and father, a family's decision to take a business public is usually driven by business concerns. For example, the capital a company needs to expand is larger than the family is willing to contribute or is capable of raising. "The dilemma is that a family chooses between the opportunity that going public provides versus giving up control and submitting to the transparency required by shareholders. Plenty of families decide to slow the company's growth in exchange for retaining control. The decision is driven by the dynamics of the industry and competitive factors."

Families can still retain influence and control over the company, says Lansberg, with the caveat that it depends on the amount of ownership still in the family. "I would say 30 percent is the breaking point. Below that, the family influence begins to wane."

Diversifying risk and providing liquidity for family needs are two of the most common reasons for taking a family company public, notes Lansberg. Often, the money gained from public sale is fanned out to individual family members, with some pooled together to provide for the future of the family. "If there is a commitment to collaborate into the future, the family may opt to manage money together to take advantage of economies of scale," he says. A family office is a typical solution, offering families the chance not only to combine their financial resources, but also to develop, with the help of experts, their intellectual and human capital.

This is an option that David Hughes is considering now that he has determined the path of the business, and is phasing it out of the family. For one thing, he worries about the fate of his teenage children with relation to the wealth his family business has bestowed on the family. He wants them to be educated about money and to be able to pursue their careers outside the cocoon of the family company in which he grew up. On the other hand, he wants them to understand and appreciate the source of the family's fortune. This dilemma and its solutions will be discussed in Chapter 6.

Once a company is public, a new concern emerges about how to handle family members who want to retain their positions in the business. The family name may still grace the company letterhead, but the firm is now answerable to outside shareholders, who demand that all opportunities for leadership among family and nonfamily employees are treated equally. This is especially tricky as the family's ownership stake diminishes along with their ownership of stock. David Hughes is facing this challenge.

Hughes sees himself as the last family member at the helm and says he is now moving through the same business progression as his father did, from president and CEO to chairman. In 1972, at age 28, he became president and his father became chairman and CEO. Two years later, Hughes moved on to become CEO as well as president, with his father remaining as chairman. Hughes's brother and cousin continued to work for the company. In the meantime, the family had been selling more stock, and currently owns less than 10 percent interest in Hughes Supply. The firm was initially listed on Nasdaq and in 1984 moved to the New York Stock Exchange, where Hughes was at one time the youngest CEO of a NYSE company.

Hughes achieved another milestone for the company last year when he hired the first president from outside the firm, even though there were family members who wanted the job. "We always had a strict policy of promotion from within," says Hughes, "and that created a great esprit de corps and a family feeling in the company, which is good. I just got to the point where I had to choose a successor, and after thirty years saw that we needed new ideas from the outside."

Although members of the next generation of Hughes's family expressed an interest in leading Hughes Supply, he encountered the typical problem that befalls subsequent generations in an unbroken line of family members who have run a company. Namely, a sense of entitlement even if they aren't up to the challenge of running the company. This is a sticky family situation that requires sensitivity. As discussed earlier, clear and objective policies developed by the family council will help mitigate any difficulty within the family because they will provide guidance for those who want a position in the company. The more the company adheres to businesslike guidelines, and doesn't view itself as a repository for anyone in the family who wants a job, the easier it will be to avoid problems.

The flip side to this particular challenge has nothing to do with the incompetence of family leaders, but everything to do with the family name. In some family companies that employ family and non-family employees and managers, it is nearly impossible for family members to receive constructive performance reviews. Their name alone precludes objectivity, and the result can be twofold. Nonfamily supervisors are afraid to be honest about faults for fear of retribution from family members in a position of authority; or they (family or nonfamily supervisors) are unduly harsh in their review because they expect a family member to deliver more.

Dennis Jaffe says that the role of an heir in a public company is highly visible and political. The apprenticeship of the successor is open for the entire company to critique, and other employees view the successor with skepticism if the person has not yet proven himself. For this reason, Jaffe recommends that the family successors cut their teeth outside the family company, or work their way up within the company, as David Hughes did, before they move to a leadership position.

To navigate through the challenges of a public company that employs family members, Ivan Lansberg recommends a small committee that goes beyond the family council to include the human resources director, the CEO, the chairman of the board, and perhaps one or two family directors "who recognize that family members cause unique issues in a family business."

The committee provides an extra measure of security for the family, because it is one step removed from the family council. And because it is composed of key decision makers in the business and family members, it can render the objectivity that a family council might have more difficulty doing. In this way, the founder and other family members can largely stay out of the fray if family members must be fired or passed over for promotion. The damage to the family dynamic is minimized because a committee that is already in place reviews the family member. The committee will be responsible for enforcing a set of rules for hiring, retaining, and firing family members, much like the family council would be if it acted in that role. "The actual rules don't matter, what matters is that they put in place a set of norms and a governance structure," says Lansberg.

On a positive note, family members who do make the cut and stay in the business can provide an enormous cultural morale boost. There are many families who use their link to the founder's name to their advantage. The Ford Motor Company is an example of a firm that has managed to largely retain family stewardship. Although the company had an outside CEO for twenty years, William Clay Ford, great-grandson of Henry Ford, became the next CEO, providing a family face to go with the famous name.

Successful business transitions are dependent on the founder's ability to plan for and accept change. As we have seen, there are many ways to relinquish control—the key is that the founder sets up the vision, but allows the next generation to modify it and live out its own dreams. The benefits of a family business come from the melding of family and business goals, and from the riches afforded to the family for its further development of intellectual and human capital. However, the same business ties that bind may choke if pulled too tightly by the founder. As families morph through the generations, writing additional chapters in the narrative, both company and family will end up stronger when they forge new and different bonds together.

In the next chapter, we'll examine how the founder and family adjust once the business has been sold. What new opportunities and dilemmas will the family encounter and how can they keep the narrative alive?

Chapter 2 Two

Keeping
Future Generations
Connected

THE DILEMMA:

*I sold my business at the right time and have more
than enough to take care of my family, but I feel alone
and uncomfortable in my new position of wealth. What
do I do with my time, and how do I preserve a connection with the family wealth in subsequent generations?*

EVEN WITHOUT SUCCESSION planning, letting go of a business
and transitioning to a new life can be fraught with tension. After
building one or more successful businesses, the role of bystander
can seem formidable for ambitious type A personalities. Founders
who retained the energy and drive it took to build the business have
to find an outlet as they face a new dilemma. They developed a business that yielded more wealth than they ever dreamed of, but now
feel that their identity and sense of purpose are gone. The next generation has also lost some of its connection with the family identity
and must write its own chapters in the family narrative, which will
include the history of the business and the legacy of its wealth.

The entire family is seeking a new identity, away from its former
connection to the day-to-day operations of the founder's life's work.

The family will now take a new direction together, with the family business history as the foundation and the money from the sale as the enabler. The family has wealth it can use to enrich the dreams of everyone, but first it must understand the transition it is going through and take steps to preserve its family heritage. In this chapter, we will examine the following issues:

- Redefining the role: The founder must exit his business with a plan for what to do next.
- Remembering the rest of the family: Everyone is affected by the sale of the business.
- Keeping the past alive: Family's challenge is to chronicle its business history once the company is no longer in the family.

An Entrepreneur's Story

Steve Ross (not his real name) remembers a defining moment of his "retirement" at age 41. Without a 40-hour-plus workweek to anchor his schedule, he had lost his usual frame of reference. "The weekend would come and I would wonder how I could enjoy it when I didn't work all week," he says. "What was so special about Friday night?"

An entrepreneur who had built two successful businesses, Ross retired at an age when most men are paying hefty mortgages and contributing to college funds for their children. While loath to use the word retirement, Ross first stepped back from his day-to-day life running a business when his twin children were in first grade. Although Ross says he realized early in his career that he wanted the business to work for him rather than the other way around, the conversion to a life of relative leisure still took him by surprise. "It was about a year's transition," he says, "and I didn't enjoy it the way I could have because there was some anxiety." If he had to do it again, he says, he would have "actively jumped into a recreational mode," playing more golf and tennis. "I would have said, 'this is a time you may not get back, so enjoy it.'"

Ross maintains that he didn't intend for his business to be a family legacy, yet the loss of the tangible evidence of his drive required a new way of thinking. "I looked at the business more as a tool to create a liquidity event. Then I wasn't so attached to it that I couldn't sell it." Once the business was gone, not only did he have to fill his time, but he also worried about instilling a work ethic in his children while he himself was not working. "It was a huge challenge to find meaning and fulfillment in nonfinancial activities," he says.

Compounding matters, in 1990, he moved his family from the small white-collar town where his businesses were located to an area of Florida with more retirees. "It was a cultural shift," he says. "In our small town, if you went out to play golf at the club on a Tuesday morning, people would gossip. Where we are now, if you go to work on a Tuesday morning, people will gossip." Eventually, Ross became involved in businesses that both intrigued him and provided his children with a memorable example of hard work.

Now that the twins are young adults on the brink of post-college plans, his apprehension has shifted to transferring his fortune. "It's the classic case of if I give my kids too much money, am I going to ruin them, and how much is too much?" Ross has overcome this particular fear by informing his children that he and his wife are bequeathing much of their wealth to the family foundation. His children have been involved in setting up the foundation and in the decisions about how the foundation money will be allocated. The couple also introduced their children to budgets; even requiring them to keep weekly budgets while they were in college and to submit written requests for cash from their modest trust funds.

Ross understands that his next most important role is as teacher and mentor to the next generation as well as legacy builder. He is pursuing his new roles with the same vigor he maintained while building his businesses. Finding a new role is critical to the founder's continued productivity in the family, but if the children are grown, founders may have a more difficult time defining a purpose.

Redefining the Role

As Steve Ross discovered, the first step for founders who have sold a business is to figure out what the next phase of their lives will encompass. At first, they may feel adrift. "One founder told me, 'I feel like a general who has just retired,'" says Gerald Le Van, a family wealth mediator with Le Van Company. "They are now in the business of investment. They used to manufacture widgets. They are strangers in a strange land and need outside help, unless they want to do it themselves," he says.

Those type A founders, who just can't seem to stop, sometimes evolve into serial entrepreneurs, starting new and different businesses because they can't envision a life without the structure that being a leader requires. The money from the sale of the original company may give them the opportunity to try a business they always wanted to lead. A car dealer may become a restaurateur, for example. The double challenge here is to avoid risking too much of the original wealth on a new venture and to allow the entire family to take on roles that will broaden their intellectual and human capital.

For the "once an entrepreneur, always an entrepreneur" founder who doesn't want the regimen of running a new start-up, mentoring a next-generation entrepreneur might prove a fruitful use of his talent. We'll discuss this more in Chapter 3. Founders should understand, however, that in this role they should not impose their will on the new entrepreneur, but rather lend their wisdom and experience.

Those founders who prefer to veer away from the company life will find a range of pursuits outside the business world, says Joan DiFuria, cofounder of Money, Meaning & Choices. "We find people who sell the company and turn to mentoring others, get involved in managing their own portfolios, or serve on boards." Emulating the European attitude is a good place for retiring founders to start, she adds. "[Europeans] have a greater sense of ease about life. They certainly work hard, but they take pleasure in life—morsels of pleasure from food, from relationships, and from living. In general, I think they have an easier time, whereas Americans are on high speed. In America, our icons have always been those who make a lot of money."

Taking pleasure in his accomplishment is part of what Jim Liautaud is doing as he brings to life his image of a united family who uses its financial capital as a catalyst. The Liautauds have always been in agreement on one point—they want to remain close. And Liautaud has worked hard to achieve his vision of a place where his children and grandchildren can gather to enjoy one another's company. He expanded his father's retreat in Wisconsin to provide a camp for his family and for future generations to spend their summers. There, the children can live and play together, building lifetime memories. "[The camp] plays a big part in our lives," he says.

Liautaud devotes himself to instilling the family legacy of values that are focused on providing a healthy and supportive environment for the grandchildren, which in turn gives incentive for the family to be gracious to each other. His passions include actively promoting philanthropy in the family name, and writing poetry and essays chronicling moments and events of family history. "I am now living Cicero's fourth season of life," he says, "overindulging in all the low-hanging fruits of my past life, living it totally selfishly, and only with those I cherish and love the most."

Experts applaud this approach to preserving the family narrative. Jay Hughes, for example, takes a philosophical view of the role of the first generation when it retires and subsequent family members come of the age of responsibility. "The Hindus believe that our path in this life is to evolve to a deeper place in the universe, and to live each stage fully and completely," he says. "So the day your first grandchild is born, you can begin to live the third stage of life, which is spiritual development."

Remembering the Rest of the Family

Discovering a new role for the founder is not the only transition occurring within the family when a business is sold. The entire clan is adjusting to the loss of the family identity and is contemplating new chapters of the narrative. The opportunities to use the wealth for philanthropy, new and different entrepreneurial pursuits, or simply more quality family time are exciting, but the element of unknown causes anxiety.

What is going through the mind of the founder's spouse when the founder sells the business? "The wife is afraid he's going to be home for lunch every day and their life will be disrupted," says Lee Hausner. "On the other hand, she's excited because now they can have the life she has always wanted but couldn't have while he was building the business." And what about the children? They are wondering if they will profit financially from the sale. Without the business as anchor, the family has to work together to define roles. "This is a time when the philanthropic initiatives of the family can become the unifying force and family foundations often serve as the unifying function of the operating business," says Hausner.

Families should seize this opportunity to form a family council, if one is not already in place, suggests Le Van. "A lot of families find this fun," he adds. "So often the business is the family identity, the community image. It's the heritage, so now who are we? We are a rich family without a company, and we have to redefine ourselves." The family council will help direct the family's new path and identity.

A successful family council, he says, coordinates wealth with the family's relational estate—that complex web of DNA, history, heritage, and interpersonal and interdependent relationships that connects them across the generations. The council in this instance acts as the family's new company. The family decides who will be on the council, whether to include in-laws, former spouses, uncles, aunts, cousins, or domestic partners. The family proceeds to redefine itself and decide what to do with the wealth. Deciding how to manage the family's wealth is another opportunity for the family council to be active. (For more discussion on the family council, see Part II.)

If the family decides to pursue its charitable interests, various relatives can take on new roles and enhance their relationship to one another by determining philanthropic initiatives to enhance the family legacy. Some may want to investigate potential areas for charitable giving, while others will develop policies or a family website for grant writers and for the public to visit.

If the management of the wealth is the new family business, qualified and interested family members may want the position of chief investment officer, determining the best investments for the family. Others may want to act as financial officer or they may form a venture capital committee to invest in new businesses. If the wealth is meant to be passed on to the next generation, the greatest hazard is unprepared heirs, which can put a stop to the best-laid plans (discussed in greater detail in Chapter 6). "I want everyone in the family to be responsible financially," says Hausner. That means the council will have to develop fiscal education curricula and mentor children in financial responsibility and readiness.

As a starting point for families to determine how ready they are to transfer wealth to the next generation, wealth consultants Roy Williams and Vic Preisser have developed a ten-item checklist for wealth transition, which is available in their book, *Preparing Heirs*, and also on their website (www.thewilliamsgroup.org). The checklist is designed so that families can compare their responses to those of the 3,250 families that Williams and Preisser studied in order to determine what differences existed between successful post-transition families and unsuccessful ones. Williams's research notes that the questions are directly linked to successful post-transition wealth. The more "yes" answers, the more the family is like those families who were well prepared to transfer the family fortune. The questionnaire does not collect answers from all family members, but is designed to reflect an individual's perception of the family dynamic. By responding to the items, family members have a guide as to how well prepared they are.

The questionnaire is an assessment of sorts, and can help families get a grip on their condition so they can devise a plan for moving forward. Perhaps more fiscal education is needed in the family so the future generation learns budgeting and stewardship. Perhaps the family needs to communicate better and more often in order to understand its values and goals. These topics are all discussed further in Parts II and III.

Transition Checklist   ©2003 The Williams Group
(Written as Positive Affirmations rather than Questions)

1. Our family has a mission statement that spells out the overall purpose of our wealth.
2. The entire family participates in most important decisions, such as defining a mission for our wealth.
3. All family heirs have the option of participating in the management of the family's assets.
4. Heirs understand their future roles, have "bought into" those roles, and look forward to performing in those roles.
5. Heirs have actually reviewed the family's estate plans and documents.
6. Our current wills, trusts, and other documents make most asset distributions based on heir readiness, not heir age.
7. Our family mission includes creating incentives and opportunities for our heirs.
8. Our younger children are encouraged to participate in our family's philanthropic grant decisions.
9. Our family considers family unity to be just as important as family financial strength.
10. We communicate well throughout our family and regularly meet as a family to discuss issues and changes.

Keeping the Past Alive

When a family sells a business, subsequent generations won't know much about its history if the family doesn't record it. The family's challenge, therefore, is to chronicle its business history once the business is no longer in the family, and the commitment to compile that record needn't always come from the founder.

After a company is out of the family, either because it has been sold or has gone public, the final challenge is preserving the family history for future generations who played no part in building the wealth. The history is important because it is an anchor for the family—the story of the founder providing the financial resources for the family to fulfill its legacy. Inheritors want and need to understand where the

Scoring: Families able to answer "yes" to seven or more items are closely correlated with those families that have successfully transitioned their wealth. They are most likely the one family in three that will transition their values and their wealth effectively, while preserving a family unified in its belief that the individuals in the family are just as important as the wealth in the family.

Families that are able to answer "yes" to four to six items are likely to benefit substantially from efforts to improve the levels of trust and communication within their family, which is fundamental to preparing their heirs for wealth and responsibility. In the absence of a substantial effort, however, this group will remain most closely correlated with the 70 percent of the families who do not effectively transition their wealth. This is the "high return" group that can achieve the largest improvement in their transition odds of success with the least amount of work.

Families that are able to answer "yes" to only three or fewer are closely correlated to those families who failed to successfully transition their wealth and values. Those families are characterized by a dissipation of wealth among heirs, infighting and hostility within the family, and a loss of family unity in subsequent generations. It should be clearly understood that those situations could be changed for the better. It is simply a matter of family leadership and professional coaching to make the changes necessary to increase the odds for a successful transition. For this group, a substantial amount of work is required.

wealth came from and what the founder achieved in order to set the family on its current path. Sometimes it is the retired founder who takes on the compilation task, as in the case of Jim Liautaud. Other times, it is someone from a generation that is removed from the business, but who understands and appreciates the value of what was accomplished and seeks a way to keep the legacy alive.

Colleen Donaldson (not her real name) is a fourth-generation member of a family business that is dissolving. Although no one in her generation participated at a senior level in the family firm, Donaldson says the family business influenced their career paths and work ethic. Her father and uncles all served in senior executive positions in the firm and her generation had plenty of role models. "I would say that in most family businesses, there is no clear understanding of the family businesses' complete history," says Donaldson.

"We have different perspectives depending on age, exposure, and level of involvement in the business. Some stories are myth, some are reality, but we don't really know until we share with each other."

Donaldson's family journey began just before the turn of the twentieth century with her great-grandfather's foray into the lumber business. Like most entrepreneurs, he was a visionary, buying large tracts of land where a railroad was being developed. As the lumber business grew, he diversified into many other ventures, including agriculture, hotels, and various service industries. In recent years, with the impending transition of the business, Donaldson and the family have become increasingly interested in capturing the family business history. Family members gained a better understanding of the ups and downs of the family business by researching and constructing the family's genogram, making inquiries of longtime employees of the firm, and compiling a list of awards and recognitions from newspaper clippings.

In Donaldson's family, the decision to liquidate the business is multifaceted, but the driving forces are the family's interest in making the transition and the lack of interest on the part of the next generation to lead the business forward. Yet the heritage and legacy is important to the next phase of development for Donaldson and her family. It grounds them in their family roots, she notes. "Codifying our history provides a touchstone for future generations to be able to understand and appreciate the hard work and toil of our ancestors."

Donaldson doesn't want to lose her affinity to her family's wealth creation. "The business was like another member of the family because it was so pervasive," she says. Many of her family stories were known only by her grandfather. "He passed them on to my father and I would often ask him about it because I find it really fascinating. Now that my grandfather has passed on, a lot of these memories reside only with my father."

While cleaning her grandparent's attic, she discovered a journal belonging to her grandfather, written when he was a boy of 13. It revealed his adventures with his father as they traveled across the country on business. "It was cowboys and Indians time," laughs Donaldson. "It was interesting to read these personal accounts because it puts our country's history in perspective through a personal lens from our family. Through personal effects, diaries, oral traditions, family gatherings and celebrations we share some of these stories." The challenge, she adds, is to document them so they can be disseminated for generations to come. Donaldson's grandfather also wrote other memories, sharing insight for subsequent generations. She proposed to the family that they aggregate the stories that each has heard or experienced over the years in order to preserve them for the future generations. "There are pieces of history locked in everyone's closet, attic, and in each of our minds. I'm interested in getting the key to unlock these stories."

Using their resources to continue to strengthen the family narrative after the source of the wealth is gone sometimes requires greater commitment and focus from the founder and the family. Once the common ground—the business—is sold, it is easy for the family to fracture into individual units, each with a share of the pot. If the mission and vision are to remain unified, the family needs to understand its common history, even with each new generation busily writing its own separate chapter in the narrative.

"Families that have a commitment to a shared vision will create conditions that allow for members—even fourth-generation members who live out in Wyoming—to feel connected to the family," says Ivan Lansberg. "This is the byproduct of family meetings, family councils, foundations, or family offices. They broaden the family roles and allow members to be part of a larger network of people." Family meetings as a way to unite a family's members are discussed in Chapter 4.

This connection to the founder, as wealth generator, is powerful and gives heirs in the third and fourth generations, who might never have known the patriarch and matriarch, an understanding of the struggles they went through to build the wealth, and the dreams they envisioned for their offspring. In the next chapter, we'll look at how the family can help its own would-be entrepreneurs begin their narrative. By investing in family members with financial capital, these rising entrepreneurs will sustain the family for generations to come.

Chapter 3 Three

Future
Wealth Generators

THE DILEMMA:

As the family grows, the original fortune is not enough to support everyone. How can I support and encourage future wealth generators to add to the family coffers?

AT THE BEGINNING of our family narratives, when founders toiled to make a better widget, they dreamed of intellectual professions for their progeny—lawyers, doctors, professors, and the like. Such was the case with David Hughes in Chapter 1, who became a lawyer before making a career turn and entering the family business near the bottom and working his way up to chairman.

In their reveries for the next generation, what some founders fail to take into account is that future business entrepreneurs are vital for wealthy families because it is through the sale of a successful company that much of the great wealth in this country is earned. These supplemental fortunes help to offset the original asset base that is being depleted as the family grows, simply through the care and feeding of too many mouths. While the family begins to write a multigenerational narrative that will be funded through the wealth created by the founder, the money is being stretched to pay for more members who come into the fold. New family entrepreneurs are needed to replenish the financial capital.

In families like the Liautauds (discussed in Chapter 1), a flair for business seems to be evidence of genetic typecasting—would-be entrepreneurs have no interest in other professional pursuits and are not thwarted by obstacles. In essence, they act just like first-generation wealth builders. Unlike the original founders, however, the new generation of entrepreneurs has a history of successful wealth creation to draw on, leading founders to new and rewarding roles as coaches or mentors. Rising family entrepreneurs also have access to the original base of financial capital, and shrewd founders will realize that this capital can benefit the family "bank" and fund the development of future generations.

Families don't need to invest a lot to boost a determined entrepreneur. Ten years ago, Jimmy John Liautaud fueled his disappointment at not being named successor to his family's business with an "I'll show him" attitude. At the age of 18, armed with a loan of $23,871 from his father, Jim Liautaud Sr., he started his own business while still in college. Now in his early 40s, Jimmy John Liautaud is a success. His eponymous gourmet sandwich shop has 300 locations around the country, with 50 to 60 in the Chicago area alone. The loan was structured so that Liautaud Sr. owned 48 percent of the business, but Jimmy John Liautaud bought out his father's interest at the beginning of the third year. The deal worked out well for both parties. His father "tripled his original investment," says Jimmy John Liautaud. Meanwhile, he admits that for his part, "there is no way I could have started the business without the loan."

When families lend to their own, they accomplish two important objectives: they encourage and support the next generation in its dreams and they add to the family coffers. In this chapter we'll examine the following issues:

- *Depleting the fortune:* Simple math tells the "rags to riches to rags in three generations" story.
- *Professionalizing the process:* Venture capital committees help families maintain business atmosphere.

- *Mentoring the next generation:* The founder can offer invaluable guidance for new entrepreneurs.

Depleting the Fortune

Let's begin with a sobering look at the numbers. A little straightforward math lesson reveals how families are in danger of losing wealth through the generations when there is no new crop of entrepreneurs to feed the fire. As Hap Perry, founder and chairman of Asset Management Advisors, explains, "If you start out with $100 million and have four kids, and they have four kids, you're down to one sixteenth per child. Assuming a 10 percent return, with 4 percent going to taxes and 3 percent to inflation, you can't spend more than 3 percent of your assets and still have any growth in the portfolio."

Perry adds that if all sixteen children are supporting themselves in high style on a single capital base, the money will be drained in short order, especially if each child takes his or her individual share to be managed separately. Encouraging families to pool their money so they can take advantage of more sophisticated financial strategies and retain a larger capital base helps keep the fortune intact, but it's ultimately not enough to fund a growing family.

The numbers can get even worse if the families fail to consider erosion to the original capital base as the founder moves from building a business to living off the capital. Most entrepreneurs, Perry notes, aren't thinking about how expenses affect future generations when they first come into their wealth. "They spend their lives as entrepreneurs, keeping their salaries low, living in a modest house, feeding the business. All of a sudden, payday comes when they sell their business and have $100 million or more, which is more than most people dream about."

If founders proceed to step up their lifestyle, let's say by spending $30 million on houses, yachts, and private jets, they are setting themselves up for a downward cycle. "Now, the problem is instead of working off a $100 million capital base, they are working off $70 million and their expense levels have multiplied considerably to maintain the new assets," Perry says.

The immediate need is for an additional influx of financial capital, but there is also an opportunity for families to gain certain intangible benefits that deserve mention. When a family makes a financial loan or grant to one of its members, it is fostering the entire family's growth as well as that of its individual members. Perry refers to the John Adams quote cited earlier to explain further (paraphrased here): "I must study politics and war that my sons may have liberty to study mathematics and philosophy ... in order to give their children a right to study paintings and poetry ..."

"It's a question of family cohesiveness," Perry explains. "The odds of success for multiple generations are higher if the family supports all its constituencies—the soldiers, farmers, and poets." Founders should expect and want to promote future generations of "soldiers," who become the next generation of the entrepreneurs, with a loan that will be repaid to the family in future financial (as well as human and intellectual) assets. They will also want to use their wealth to support the "poets" with grants in order to increase the family's intellectual and human capital, though perhaps not its monetary capital. Perry calls this outlook "managing the poet-soldier mix" and likens it to families deciding to invest portions of their fortune in venture capital via loans and portions in philanthropy through grants. When families understand this concept, they find a way to support everyone's vision, both financially and otherwise.

Because money provides the means to that vision, supporting entrepreneurship is vital. As an example of a family who supported the next generation of entrepreneurs, Perry describes a client who sought to fund his son's start-up venture, a business that was far from the founder's own area of expertise. The founder, having missed the opportunity to obtain funding from his own entrepreneurial father, wanted to support his son's attempt at business. A relatively small loan was arranged, with payment not due until the business had a chance to gain solid footing. This is where the loan diverged from that which a typical bank would make and became an important element of encouragement and trust in the next generation. By giving the son a chance to build the business before payment was due, the founder was expressing enormous confidence in his son's abilities.

Perry says the deal also gave the founder a chance to work on the family's mission and values. By deciding the terms of the deal as a unit, and determining how to support the new venture, the family was carrying out both its value of nurturing the goals of individual family members and its mission of encouraging entrepreneurship.

Professionalizing the Process

How should families structure themselves to encourage entrepreneurial quests and increase financial capital? Family venture committees, created for the purpose of investing in new family start-ups by lending money to entrepreneurs, are an effective way to do it. These committees are sometimes part of the family council.

The committee convenes to set parameters for loans and guidelines for what is expected of applicants, including who in the family is eligible (spouses, for example), purpose of the loan, age of applicant, level of experience, limits of the loan, repayment terms, and roles of family council members, should the need arise. The committee should have a written policy for applicants to review so that there are no surprises and no future accusations of being treated differently from another family member. Some families seek outside counsel to draft these policies if they don't have experts within the family. Even though the family is making the loan, the agreements should be formal and in writing and include the amount of the loan, interest rate, collateral, and payment terms. A cautionary note: The IRS will calculate imputed interest if it deems a loan among family members to be interest-free or if the interest rate is unusually low. The lender will be responsible for the taxes due on the phantom interest income. If there is no interest charged, the IRS will treat the phantom interest as a gift and apply it toward the lender's annual gift tax exclusion.

The entrepreneur, or borrower, is responsible for providing regular business reports to the committee, including all financials. In essence, he or she is being kept at arm's length and families would do well to remember that the transaction is a business arrangement even though they are dealing with a family member. The business plan from the entrepreneur has to include the potential risks, financial projections, market analysis, competitors' forecasts, and the entrepreneur's qualifications.

Even when all these recommendations are followed, there is still a risk. As any business founder knows, not all start-ups succeed. In fact, a startling number fail within the first few years. Before the loan is granted, the committee must carefully consider the ramifications of investing in a venture that might fail. Losing money is one thing, losing a family member due to bitterness over money is quite another.

The objectivity afforded by the written policy, as well as a written agreement regarding the specific terms of the deal, will help families preempt any emotional outbursts in the event the start-up crashes. The next step, of course, is for the family to support and guide the wounded entrepreneur into more fruitful pursuits in the future. If the committee has properly prepared itself for this outcome, it will have designated specific roles to family members and researched the actions they should take. This leads naturally into mentoring, an essential role for family members who want to see their hard-earned wealth preserved in subsequent generations.

Mentoring the Next Generation

When families provide financial backing for new entrepreneurs, they are investing only a portion of their pooled resources. There is also an opportunity to contribute talent in other areas, for example, as coaches and mentors. These are particularly good roles for the founder, who might be seeking an outlet for his wisdom and experience. In the ideal situation, young would-be entrepreneurs learn business principles at the feet of the founder and later enjoy a mentoring relationship as the seeds of the new business take hold and grow. The founder retains a valuable role when he leaves the business and his expertise will be appreciated by a new generation. After all, with a successful founder already in the family, why keep that talent locked in a vault, limiting the family to a one-time-only success?

In the relationship between founder and rising entrepreneur, the new businessperson gains insight beyond a business school degree. By taking advantage of the knowledge and acumen of the founder, as well as that of others on the family council who can provide training, the new entrepreneur increases his probability of success in a sector with a notoriously bad track record.

There is an important distinction to be made here between a mentor and a coach, and it is vital for determining how the founder and the entrepreneur will proceed in their relationship. A coach is dedicated to improving skills. A mentor, on the other hand, goes beyond teaching to ask the hard questions that no one else will ask, and expects the person he is mentoring to figure out the answers. The coach is the teacher; the mentor is the guide or trusted counselor. Thus, the mentor is the more valuable role because it forces rising entrepreneurs to expand their thinking "outside the box."

The danger for the founder in taking on the role of a coach or teacher is that he may revert to thinking his way is the best or only way, and that would be disastrous for the new entrepreneur. Too much meddling by the first generation, as we saw in Chapter 1, is dangerous for those attempting to run a business on their own. Better to be the wise and trusted elder who counsels the future business-person, imparting knowledge in a way that allows the entrepreneur to discover his own solutions. The mentor-entrepreneur relationship will work only if the entrepreneur sets boundaries, and both parties commit to those boundaries. If the relationship slops over into one of parent-child, for example, it is the fault of the child for not clearly defining the boundaries and holding the parent to them.

There are times, however, when the entrepreneur still seeks a parent-child conversation, and in that instance, both parties must be clear as to what is expected so they can respond appropriately. When relationship boundaries are unambiguous and separate, there are no misunderstandings about the type of advice being given by the founder, or that being sought by the entrepreneur.

Families follow different stages of mentoring and teaching as the next generation grows into its business roles, says Dennis Jaffe. They may begin with teaching and coaching of skills, and evolve into true counseling and mentoring roles. Jaffe describes the stages as follows:

1) The first generation strives to create a work ethic and a sense of passion and drive in their children so they don't have "a sense of apathy."

2) The first generation helps the second develop skills, "not just pushing them all to go to business school, but encouraging them to do what they want, and to show them what's possible." Families at this stage begin talking to their offspring about what they want to do in life. "Some people will go in other directions, but some will see the business as an opportunity." If the family business wins out, good communication is crucial, Jaffe says. "Families can't give mixed messages about what's expected." This is the roles-defining stage discussed earlier.

3) Finally, when the next generation wants to go in another direction, with help from the family business, the decision-making process should include a board of directors (or a venture capital arm). The family and the board have to create the rules around loans granted to the start-up business and the process for review. Because the start-up business is fueled by a loan from the family business, the implication is that the start-up is part of the family enterprise, and thus subject to the same objective review by the board. The founder can then act as mentor for the child, while the board takes over the details of the business venture loan.

Joanne Carter (not her real name) and her family are going through these same stages as they begin to focus on the third generation. Carter had assumed leadership of the family enterprises after the death of her father and now the family is pondering how to encourage the third generation in entrepreneurship and stewardship of their current business. The oldest of that generation is in college and showing signs of business acumen. He has been involved in the family business in a limited way, but the board is putting certain criteria in place so that family members can begin teaching the third generation business skills. "Our kids are still fairly young," says Carter. "We haven't worked out the criteria for how we will react in supporting their ventures, but I'm sure they'll have to put forth a business plan and proposal that will be analyzed by the board, and we'll have to decide the amounts, circumstances, and terms of a loan, as well as the type of experience needed to lead a venture and the expected return."

Carter is on the right path to formalizing the process for the next generation by recognizing its interest in business and beginning to think about requirements for financial support. Families who have reached this point in their narratives are beginning to plan beyond the original founder and his single-minded vision for the expanded family and its multigenerational success. Like Carter, they are realizing that each generation takes a hand in guiding the next and that policies and procedures continually need to be developed. The earlier that family members understand their roles in managing the poet-soldier mix, the better prepared they will be to proactively promote the success of the entire family.

As families expand their knowledge and vision, their success is rooted in communication and the ability to work together. In Part II, we'll learn how successful families frame their communication structures using the base of their common core values and learn to govern themselves through the inevitable challenges that will come their way.

PART II

Retaining Family
Cohesiveness

IMAGINE THE FOLLOWING scenario: A Russian immigrant arrives in the United States in the early 1900s. He learns English by reading the daily newspaper and puts himself through law school at night. Eventually, he opens a law firm and employs his three sons. By sheer force of will, talent, and dedication, he begins a family dynasty that will reign over a vast fortune for four generations.

The founder's sons and grandsons, equally ambitious and talented, expand the family's stake in investments and acquisitions, including the Hyatt hotel chain. By the time the fourth generation comes to power, the family's wealth is in the billions of dollars, encompassing hundreds of companies and thousands of family trusts. An American success story? In terms of amassing financial riches, the answer is yes. In terms of family harmony—ultimately, no.

The family just described is that of the Pritzkers, one of the wealthiest families in the country and until recently, thought to be extremely close. What has unfolded in the last few years is a tale of lawsuits, miscommunication, and the public desecration of a once private family.

Money—managing the family's various enterprises or even just the pooled wealth—is the nexus that keeps most wealthy families together, but it can also cause destruction if the family hasn't solidified a base of communication, respect, and common values from which to operate. Miscommunication among family members at a critical point in the Pritzker family narrative was enough to set in motion a collapse that was precipitated in large part by the patriarch's inability to recognize that the family needed to chart its future as a unit and not from the point of view of a single individual.

In most wealthy families, the founder rules as a monarch because it was he who created the fortune. As we began to uncover in Chapter 1, and we'll see now in Part II, in families that have amassed the wealth, the ability to work together effectively is what will propel the clan through its various dilemmas.

Jay Pritzker, a member of the third generation, and the most recent reigning patriarch, ruled autocratically, an approach that is unpopular with just about everyone. The successful leader in business—the one who essentially takes charge and runs the operation

while the others follow—is not necessarily the same as the successful leader of families, the one who nurtures and enriches the entire
family.

Jay Pritzker, grandson of founder Nicholas Pritzker, lived relatively modestly in relation to his wealth and wanted his heirs to do
the same. He developed some health problems and was nearing
retirement when he communicated his intentions. He called a meeting of the next generation and reportedly presented a letter he had
written regarding how the family wealth should be spent.

Like wealthy families everywhere, Jay Pritzker's worries included
appointing a successor and sustaining the family mission after his
death. He wanted the next generation to be happy, but he also
wanted the family's financial empire to be in good hands. His letter
stated that the family's wealth, largely held in various trusts, was to
be used to further the family's myriad businesses and philanthropic
enterprises, not to make individual family members wealthier. He
also named his eldest son, Tom Pritzker, as his successor. Lastly,
he requested that the family honor his wishes. In essence, Jay
Pritzker was imposing his own values on the rest of the family and
when those present at the meeting didn't voice any objections, he
assumed their silence signaled acceptance. This was a fatal error for
his family's unity.

Jay Pritzker died in 1999, and on a cold January day in Chicago,
Tom Pritzker delivered a moving memorial tribute to his father.
Huddled together in the congregation were nearly all fifty-two sur-
viving members of the family and close to one thousand friends and
associates. Tom Pritzker intoned his father's belief that "a man's only
immortality comes from the values he instilled in his children."

Soon after that day of apparent familial accord, the seeming
serenity erupted into a morass of lawsuits and bitter accusations. The
source of the lawsuits was an unlikely person, one of the teenage heirs.
The wealth that had grown steadily into a multibillion-dollar fortune,
tended by four generations to support Jay Pritzker's mission of philanthropy, had splintered and a previously close-knit family was blown
to bits. The death of the patriarch had snapped the fragile bonds that
had weakened through several generations of brewing resentment.

Liesel Pritzker, age 19 at the time, sued her father, Robert Pritzker (Jay Pritzker's brother), and all the Pritzker cousins. Her 20-year-old brother, Matthew Pritzker, joined her in the suit. They contended that their father had raided their trust funds. The story continued to unfold and later revelations included a ten-year plan among some members of the fourth generation to break up the family's empire and split the fortune among themselves, thus ending the dynasty. Liesel Pritzker stated that the lawsuit was not about the cash, but about understanding what was happening to her money and being treated fairly. The family later settled with Liesel and Matthew Pritzker.

Friends expressed dismay that a family that had seemed so unified and private would publicly argue over money. Jay Pritzker, they believed, would have been horrified by the behavior of his progeny. How did Jay Pritzker's good intentions go awry? As leader of the family, he did his best to promote his children in business wherever they showed aptitude and desire. What he failed to do, however, was to recognize that he couldn't determine the family's values and mission based solely on his beliefs, as stated in his letter to the family. The family had to do that as a group. Pritzker was a shrewd manager of the family's business, but he was not an effective leader of the family because he failed to understand that when family members suspect that their values are being ignored, they lose interest in unity.

"A statement of [one person's] intentions is usually not enough for a family to support a monumental decision about family wealth," says Hap Perry. "It's really all about teamwork and communication." Without an understanding of the underlying values of the founding generation, families lose the common thread that binds them, and as Jay Hughes notes, it is almost never the wealth generator, or controller of the wealth, who sees the defensiveness and resentment within the family. "Typically, it's the next generation, or two down, that perceives that there are issues that need to be resolved while the matriarch and patriarch are still alive," he says. When the family didn't openly discuss Jay Pritzker's letter at that meeting, they lost the opportunity to come to agreement as a family.

When some of the most financially successful families fail to maintain family harmony, how can the rest of us expect to succeed? Through a dedicated and ongoing effort at communication, experts say, beginning with the discovery of the values of each individual, as well as those of the family as a whole. Why are values so important? Because every person's judgments and subsequent actions are a result of those personally held values and beliefs. Therefore, when a family's mission and operating procedures come from shared core values, the chances of remaining a cohesive unit are greatly increased. Families that begin by talking and listening, from the foundation of their common core values, and continue to practice those communication skills throughout the inevitable changes of direction that families encounter, will find it easier to preserve all three forms of capital: financial, human, and intellectual.

There will be crises involving the wealth as the family journeys through the generations, as we will see in Chapter 4 when we look at some common governance problems. But if the family has developed its mission as a means to carry out its values, and has learned how to communicate and govern, it will have a better chance of beating the odds. It is critical for wealthy families to understand and practice their missions if they want to sustain the fortune. Again, brilliant steerage of a business enterprise, as in the case of the Pritzkers, is not the same as nurturing and guiding a family through its multigenerational development.

Fortunately, the desire among families to maintain cohesiveness is hardwired. "There's a strong urge in relatives to stay together to share their family history," says Lee Hausner. But don't expect miracles overnight, she cautions. The process of family communication spans generations and laying the groundwork early for effective decision-making and openness is worth the effort. "Learning the skills to communicate is the most important thing a family can do," Hausner claims. Families need to take the necessary steps, and in the proper order, to maintain cohesiveness. As we'll see in Chapter 4, some type of family meeting is the best way to accomplish these steps:

1) Discuss and agree on the values of the family as the basis for all further development of its financial, human, and intellectual capital.

2) Write a mission statement as a means to carry out the values.
3) Create a governance structure to fit the family's needs.
4) Guide the subsequent generations.

Later, in Chapter 5, we consider a common dilemma that can threaten family harmony: the introduction of a new spouse. When this new person, especially one of lesser financial means, comes into a wealthy family, the immediate concern is to level the financial playing field. Once that has been accomplished, the couple can move forward in the relationship unencumbered by one partner's feeling of inequality. We'll also look at specific methods to accomplish that, with particular emphasis on prenuptial agreements as the most universal of these methods.

Chapter Four

Keeping the
Family Together

THE DILEMMA:

I want the wealth to enhance our dreams, but don't want it to be the only reason we stay together.

THE PRITZKER CASE is a fitting example of what happens when a family is united by its financial success alone. Believing that the riches are enough to sustain them as a family, and distracted by their dazzling financial success, they are blind to the cracks in the family until a crisis erupts. If the family stays together solely to augment one another financially, it is more than likely going to fracture when each individual sees no reason not to take his share of the money and run.

A set of common values that defines the family and provides the framework for all future interaction is the first and most important step toward cohesiveness. When the family is nurtured by its values and strives to reach its full intellectual and human capacity, the financial riches become the enabler rather than the reason for being. When family members argue about money, what they're really fighting about are their differing core values. If members of the family think their values are not being compromised, they're more likely to work toward the greater good.

Families then have to communicate regularly in order to build and transfer wealth, and do it from a base of common values. As obvious as it sounds to say that families need to talk, there are so many reasons why it is difficult. Unspoken resentments and perceived judgments, different perspectives, and sibling rivalry are just a few obstacles. Many families need a process to help them get started, to remind them to continue to communicate, and to provide a framework for how the family continues to work as a unit. Families must learn to communicate as a prerequisite for working together. Family meetings afford an excellent means for open and regular discussions and for developing a common set of values as a precursor to writing a mission statement, creating governance structures, and mentoring the next generation.

In this chapter, the business plays a role in some of the governance problems, but we'll see that there are also other entities that require family communication and governance, and many versions of the operating principles the family will have to put in place. These entities, besides the family business, include management of the portfolios of wealth, vacation homes and shared land, and philanthropic endeavors. The specific issues we'll examine include:

- *Meeting face to face:* Family meetings can take different forms depending on a family's needs.
- *Guiding the family:* The mission statement solidifies the family's core values and requires everyone's buy-in.
- *Governing through problems:* Governance procedures can help the family through common crises, such as staying together following the death of the founder, dealing with unproductive family members, and property management issues stemming from the sheer number of owners.
- *Preparing the next generation:* Mentoring is most effective when it involves the entire family's efforts.

Meeting Face to Face

Let's begin with the easiest advice to give, but usually the hardest for families to do well—establish regular communication through family meetings. Family meetings can take different forms depending on a family's needs. If, as George Burns said, "Happiness is having a large, loving, caring, close-knit family in another city," then the gathering of one's clan may be limited to an annual angst-ridden Thanksgiving dinner. For many families, however, especially those with significant wealth or a family business to pass on, the need to get together goes beyond sharing a holiday meal, and regular family meetings fit the bill. Decisions about managing wealth, philanthropic enterprises, or family business need to be made. Families must learn how to govern themselves as they manage their assets, and communication is the cornerstone.

If the family business has been sold and the children are young, founders may want to prepare their future heirs by establishing regular discussions about values and money management. Multigenerational families who have several enterprises may require a more structured decision-making process, often with the help of a consultant or with the formation of a family council. We will discuss three types of meetings here.

Meetings Initiated at Home

This type of family meeting is often easiest if children are young and pliant and the parents are still in control. When these children become adults, with their own need for control, the meetings can become more difficult and as we'll see later, an outside facilitator may be needed.

Family meetings when children are young needn't be formal affairs. Gathering around the kitchen table once a week is often enough for everyone to voice opinions, learn from one another, and develop effective communication skills. As the children mature, they can continue to structure their lives around the family's core values and discuss how those values might change. Families should also use the meetings to build on the values and teach children about fiscal responsibility and community service. Money management lessons might begin with the basic concept of how currency is used, move on to the importance of budgeting when the children are older, and then on to basic investing principles and charitable giving. As young adults, the next generation will be much more prepared to inherit and manage money if it has had a fiscal education (as we'll see in Chapter 6).

Beginning the process of communication when children are young means that families will feel comfortable working together later on because they have had opportunities to practice their values as they mature. But the key, as we'll see with the Harrison family, is to be consistent.

Karen Harrison (not her real name) and her husband initiated family meetings when their two children were preteens. "We had a sacred time, 5:00 p.m. Sunday afternoon for an hour," says Harrison. The children were at an age when the parents believed it was crucial to begin talking about serious issues. "It's important not to assume that we as parents know everything." The meetings usually began with a round of compliments for everyone and then spun off into discussions about upcoming schedules, school, friendships, drugs, sex, finances, and any other matters that were critical at the time. The topics were discussed within the framework of establishing family values. "We would take a value a week and discuss it and try to figure out how to work on it. Like honesty," Harrison says. "It's a great way to instill values. If the kids went against the values, we tried to let the natural consequences occur, because that's best. But sometimes we would impose additional consequences." The result, Harrison contends, is that her children were armed with information to support the family's values. Good mental and physical health is another of the family's values. "With all the information we provided them, I would be shocked if my kids ever smoked a cigarette."

When families discuss their visions and values, the next step is to agree upon them as a unit, and state them in a way that will provide a guidepost as the family grows and faces new dilemmas. The Harrison family's list of values was a long time in development, and parents would be wise to take into account the notoriously short attention span of young children who would rather be outside on the swing set or kicking a soccer ball around the yard. The Harrisons discussed their values one at a time and took more than a year to develop their list. "We spent a lot of time on honesty," says Harrison. "That was a tough one for the kids because of all the peer pressure they had, but the consequences of being caught in a lie helped them to understand the value."

Harrison's daughter Mary, now 22, admits that the values discussed during those early years stayed with her to adulthood, but confesses to the tedium of meetings when she was young. "Yeah, I hated them," she bluntly says. "It felt like lectures. When you're a kid, you don't want to sit around and read minutes." She understands that the Sunday meetings provided a foundation of communication skills, but Mary Harrison says she personally felt the meetings were more beneficial when she was older. Even during the busy teen years, the family managed to eat breakfast and dinner together every day, and Mary notes that their schedules didn't get in the way. "We made it work."

During those mealtimes, Karen Harrison never let up. "My mom would have Ann Landers articles to show us and discuss," says Mary Harrison. In this way, the family meetings took on an even more casual atmosphere. Instead of a set time devoted to the gathering, the family remained flexible and took advantage of the mealtimes, during which they continued their discussions about values.

Karen Harrison continued to emphasize communication in the family, reinforcing the values as her children grew. They wrote semi-annual and yearly goals while still in grade school, incorporating the values learned during the family meetings. When they went off to college, Harrison and her husband drafted a set of expectations reflecting those same values, which the children signed. Honesty still topped the list, followed by the remaining values, including respect, spirituality, and wellness.

If the Harrisons seem unusually focused, to the point that some might wonder if the children were driven to rebel, experts counter that notion. Because Karen Harrison established regular communication with the children when they were young, the results are gratifying now that they are adults. Both Harrison children became well-adjusted adults, who do not ask for or expect handouts from their parents and who regularly participate in philanthropic activities. This is because the constant communication meant that everyone understood each individual's values and they developed the family's list together. Harrison acknowledges that, from her perspective, the meetings were easier when the children were living at home because they were a captive audience. "When they get older, they feel that they've learned everything already and they're not as interested." These days, their meetings are more business oriented, concerning the work of the family foundation they have established. As a result of the early training, the family comes to the meetings armed with good communication and listening skills, common values that they've shared throughout their lives, and a shared vision for their charitable works.

Wealthy families who don't have multigenerational businesses, family foundations, or multiple properties and portfolios can start with simple family meetings at home, as the Harrison family did. With just the nuclear family involved, the Harrisons' informal meetings became the building blocks for the formal board meetings of the foundation the parents wanted to establish later on. At the time they instituted their family meetings, the transference of the wealth from the sale of the husband's business was the biggest concern, and Harrison wanted to be sure her children understood how fortunate they were, and that she and her husband would be giving much of their wealth to charity. That's why the discussion of values and the subsequent list were critical for the family to develop.

Instituting family meetings at home is not difficult, but it does require some sort of format. Following are some tips for families who want to initiate family meetings:

1) Everyone is an equal at family meetings and should be treated accordingly. Even young children deserve to be heard and to feel that their suggestions are taken seriously.

2) Stick to the established time for family meetings, whether weekly or monthly. Changing the schedule will result in a lack of commitment to the meetings.

3) Give everyone a chance to speak, but don't allow the meetings to deteriorate into gripe sessions.

4) Plan for some of the meetings to take place in recreational settings to avoid giving the meetings a negative association.

5) Allow each family member the opportunity to be in charge of a meeting by rotating the "chair."

6) Compile a list of important issues to be discussed or decided at the next meeting.

7) Practice good communication skills. Describe your feelings without being defensive, speak directly and be specific, describe how other people's behavior affects you without casting blame.

8) Practice good listening skills. Don't interrupt a speaker, listen with an open mind, be sure you understand what has been said by repeating the thought back to the speaker, and ask questions that invite the speaker to elaborate.

Hiring an Outside Consultant

At this next level, family members often find that the meetings run more smoothly, and the outcomes are more agreeable, if they bring in a consultant trained in helping families work through complex family or business issues that may be intertwined with emotions.

In these situations, the family typically has not established common core values and there may be several generations and their spouses involved. The catalyst for this second type of meeting is usually an event in the family (the death of a senior family member or the decision to divide the family assets). Meetings of this type, with heightened emotional states, might lead to lots of yelling and stomping out of the room. The first order of business is to establish communication rules so that family members can be heard and can tolerate being in the same room with each other.

"Most families develop two levels of communication," says Lee Hausner. "One is the safe level, where housekeeping and scheduling items are discussed, for example. The other is considered not safe, because the emotional reaction can be too negative." "Unsafe" conversations might involve the division of family assets, differing charitable interests, health care for aging parents, or other emotionally charged issues. Trained consultants help navigate through the issues that prevent effective communication, and develop solutions the family can understand and support. To start the meetings off on the right foot, make sure everyone in the family is comfortable with and has confidence in the chosen consultant. Word of mouth is the best resource for finding trained consultants. Talk to other people who have conducted facilitated family meetings to get their recommendations. Books and websites devoted to family meetings can also provide sources. Family attorneys or financial advisers may be able to provide referrals as well. Once family members have interviewed the potential consultant and are happy with the choice, the consultant will generally begin by talking with family members both individually and as a group. "I want to know all the hot buttons beforehand, through one-on-one meetings," says Hausner. From there, the process of teaching families how to communicate as a precursor to uncovering common values begins. This includes giving family members the tools to listen effectively and to make their points without succumbing to emotion. It also means that the consultant will stop the discussion when it seems to be going off-track or is becoming too emotional.

The expert will set the rules of protocol at the first meeting so that family members know what to expect and what the boundaries are. Experts also agree that starting with simpler topics helps break the ice and enables the family to refine its communication skills before tackling the tough issues. "I often say that the first meeting isn't the first meeting. It's just trying to get to the beginning," says Jay Hughes. "That relaxes people and they realize they don't have to solve everything in one meeting."

Once civil communication is established and everyone is in agreement regarding the group's common values, the consultant helps families lay the issues on the table, and discuss them with an end goal in sight. Hausner uses a flip chart to keep track of issues at meetings. The ultimate goal is to teach the family to conduct meetings that will produce solutions for each situation, much like the way a business operates. The benefit of a consultant is that as an outsider, he or she brings an objective perspective to the meetings and can say what family members may not be able to say to each other.

Stuart Jones (not his real name) belongs to the third generation of his family. He says that he and his siblings learned the value of having meetings facilitated by a consultant. Prompted by a family issue that needed settlement, they decided some ten years ago to conduct meetings on their own. "We rented a meeting room, and at the end of the first meeting, something was said that became a harbinger of what was to come and led to raised voices and hurt feelings. In the next few years, we had varying degrees of success conducting meetings ourselves until someone suggested that we needed outside help." The family hired Jay Hughes to facilitate. "Jay brought a wonderful philosophy and gentle spirit to the meetings," Jones says. "In general, it improved the quality of our meetings by giving us focus and helped to keep us on track. Ultimately, we needed someone to be the parent."

Experts often say that families should learn to conduct themselves as they would a business in order to gain the most from the meetings. But as Jones discovered, that can be difficult. "You try, but you can't totally do that," he says. "No one wants to look at their brother or sister and say, 'you can't do that.'" The consultant, on the other hand, brings impartiality and objectivity to meetings. By being able to see the forest, and not just the trees, consultants navigate families through the crisis and in the process teach them how to foresee other potential developments that require them to convene in the future. As Hughes says, "Families can almost never see the issues until the point when they're in distress." He identifies three major milestones in a family's development that typically require a consultant's expertise:

1) An aging first generation, a busy second generation, and a rising third generation, leading to the sudden realization that there are complex joint decisions to make within the family.

2) The sale of a family business, in which a family transitions from a business family to a nonbusiness family.

3) The stress of transitioning a new relationship into the family, for example when a child marries someone of lesser financial means.

These different situations might determine which family members should attend the meetings. Perhaps it will be just the nuclear family if it involves Mom and Dad's estate. Or it might include spouses or cousins in the event of a transition of the family business, a problem concerning a shared vacation home, or investment in a family member's start-up venture. Experts often defer to families to decide who should be included. While Hausner encourages wide family participation, some families prefer to keep a tighter group. Consultants help families make the decision, but there are no hard and fast rules.

Hausner likes to include children if there are topics that are relevant to them. As in the Jones family, that sometimes results in a separate track for children or participation in only part of the meeting. If family finances are discussed among adults, for example, children may be brought in later for discussions about philanthropy. Family meetings can be an effective way to teach the next generation about the family business or foundation, financial stewardship, how a trust works, how to read financial statements, and a variety of other topics.

What about family members who refuse to participate? Hughes advises the family to proceed without them. "It's like that Samuel Beckett play, *Waiting for Godot*. If we wait for those who aren't coming, then we fail." Best to go ahead with those who are willing to try, with one of the issues being how to deal with the "no-shows." How often a family meets depends on the topics to be discussed and the complexity of the family situation. Once a year is usually sufficient, although many families meet quarterly. Family members who live far away can join the meetings by phone. Like the Jones family, certain events, or the performance of the family investments, may determine the frequency of meetings for a while. In the beginning, when the family is developing its values and mission statement, more frequent meetings are common. The consultant can drop out once the family is comfortable with its meeting structure, and the values have been agreed on and are in place. As Hausner says, "teaching a family to communicate is like teaching them to fish," with the goal eventually being independence from the teacher.

Forming a Family Council

Family councils exist to integrate the family and its enterprises. As the third model for family meetings, the council straddles both the business and the family. Family businesses may include a company, a portfolio, a foundation, a vacation home—basically any enterprise that requires family management and input. Even mentoring the next generation is a reason for the family to work together for its common good. When families get beyond the simple situation of teaching values to young children, they should establish a council to provide a more formal framework for the discussion of various family concerns. Families can set up councils with or without the help of a consultant.

Some type of family council usually exists in families with active business interests. The councils are useful because members typically establish a governing board of directors that includes family members who are active in the business and some who are not active but hold votes on the board. Meetings are conducted in a business-like manner, albeit with the familiarity that comes from speaking to a sibling rather than to an outside business associate. In this instance, it is helpful for families to expand beyond the pure business scope to recognize that the company is a family and as such, there are issues to be resolved that might not be present in a nonfamily business—such as the succession dilemmas discussed in Part I.

Family councils take their cues from the needs of the family. In complex situations involving the operation of multiple businesses and foundations, for example, the council provides oversight as well as operating procedures and guidelines for compensation, performance reviews, staffing among family members, and even the removal of unproductive members. As a unit that consists of family members, the council has a significant advantage over nonfamily governing structures in that council members pay attention to the next generation's needs, foster entrepreneurship, and nurture individual family members while keeping an eye on the success of the family. As we will see later in this chapter, and throughout the book, a family council that has done its prep work and developed sound policies and procedures can avoid many crises that arise within the family.

Although councils often come out of family business enterprises, they should still establish common core values as the first step. As the family business matures, and family members are off in far-flung places dealing with the multiple interests of the family, a different type of value-discovery session is required. At Asset Management Advisors, the firm founded by Hap Perry, the process begins with a Web-based questionnaire that each family member completes. An adviser collects and analyzes the responses to determine each individual's values and also the values the family holds in common. In this way, the discussions leap ahead because family members don't have to start the talks at "square one." They can begin with a discussion of values after the "homework" has been done.

By examining a variety of topics, the questionnaire reveals how the family operates as a unit and what values the individual members hold near and dear, as well as each member's perspective on the family (which may be different from that of the founder's). The values are the building blocks for further discussion and development of all generations. The questionnaire ultimately facilitates the discussion of the family's common values, leading to the mission statement, and structures for governance and mentoring.

Once the values and mission statements are formalized, family councils get down to business. Members should meet regularly and conduct themselves in a businesslike manner, keeping minutes of each meeting and observing operating procedures. Ideally, all family members will be included and the council will function as an advisory group to the family enterprises, as well as a forum for airing issues pertaining to both the business and the family. As discussed in Chapter 3, committees may form to fund and nurture future generations of entrepreneurs. Other committees may be responsible for operating the family foundation or its shared vacation properties.

According to Ivan Lansberg, the council should honor the fact that all family members have a stake in the family identity. The composition of the council may change as the family itself goes through different stages, but the raison d'etre is still the family's development and enhancement of its three forms of capital: financial, human, and intellectual.

Lansberg says that there are some recurring themes in family councils, having to do with the core values and the family's relationship with its various enterprises. Often these themes come to light when the family is embroiled in a specific dilemma, but Lansberg suggests that families consider these themes and discuss them in the abstract before the immediate dilemma sets the tone (notice the establishment of values as the first item):

- What are the central values of our family?
- How do we express these values?
- What do we do if someone feels a core value is being violated?
- How can these values be preserved and taught to future generations in the business and in the family?

Developing a family plan, Lansberg says, addresses these issues and provides a strategic map for the council. The plan can include a family history, vision of the future, mission statement, and finally, the action plan to bring the vision and mission to fruition. With all family members signing off on the plan, the family becomes united in its focus.

Guiding the Family

Once families have learned how to communicate and have unearthed their shared values through whichever type of meeting they prefer, the next step is to put those values into action via a mission statement. This written statement outlines the way in which the family will live its values.

According to Hap Perry, the mission statement is a point of reference for common understanding and a map for the family's future. Mission statements are not simply a list of goals, although these may be included. They are affirmative statements reflecting the values, commitments, and priorities of the family unit and as such, each family member should have input in making sure the family's common values are represented. Once a family mission statement is complete, Perry says, "It is important to review it and make it a living breathing document." He recommends "keeping it out of the drawer" by continually talking about it during family meetings and referring to it when the family makes decisions. That is not to say that the mission statement can't, or shouldn't, be updated. As a family grows, with additional members and new ventures, the mission will have to be rewritten to continue to reflect the common goals and values of the entire family.

Family mission statements can range from simple to complex, depending on the family's stage of development. For example, first-generation wealth founders with young children will have a mission statement that differs from that of a family that consists of multiple generations operating various family enterprises. The statements take the form of the family's view of the critical issues to work toward. Harrison's family listed the values they wanted to develop as a family. She and her family might not need to include business concerns in their mission and could even list just one or two broad goals. A sample mission statement for such a family might read as follows:

> Our family will value the importance of a loving close relationship no matter how far away from one another we live. We will try to get together at least once a year for a family vacation. We will support our commitment to philanthropy by giving our time and financial resources to organizations that promote physical fitness among young people. As individuals we will incorporate our values into our lives by living as productive healthy adults.

Other mission statements are more complex, simply because the family is larger and involved in both business and family issues. The following is a sample mission statement developed by a clan with diverse business holdings, a commitment to philanthropy through a family foundation, and a rising third generation poised to take the reigns. The statement was developed with the assistance of advisers who helped the family understand its unique dilemmas.

Whatever form the mission statement takes, the value is not so much in what it proclaims, but that it has the family's underlying values in place as the result of the entire family's participation, through family discussions or through consultations with professional advisers. As the family governs itself, the mission statement will keep everyone centered on its tenets and provide an operating framework.

Our family's purpose is to develop the human, intellectual, and financial capital of our members in order to support the pursuit of each individual's life purpose, strengthen cohesiveness both within and across generations, and contribute to the betterment of society.

To develop the human, intellectual, and financial capital of our family members, we will work continually to achieve the following:

• Promotion of family members' freedom regarding choices about their life's work and participation in family enterprises.
• Preservation of our financial resources to provide our members with opportunities to pursue life dreams and enrich family capital.
• Philanthropic responsibility and the practice of giving back to society.
• Promotion of lifelong learning and growth of individual members and the family group.
• The active embracing of life.
• Creation of an environment where members can hear and understand one another's feelings and ideas.
• Communication of the values and beliefs that guide our lives.

Governing Through Problems

The action plan doesn't stop with a mission statement. Governance procedures can help the family through various common family crises. The family has now established its core values and a method for communication through its meeting format. These are critical lessons if the family is to work together and accomplish the next steps in the family's development—governance and mentoring. Families without a business to run must still find ways to govern themselves when operating a foundation, vacation home property, or the family's financial portfolios.

The family council can decide which family situations require governance and begin to appoint committees to oversee these various concerns. If everyone has agreed to the values and the mission, governance will prove easier. In a business, as we have seen, governance entails clear operating guidelines that include leadership, compensation, hiring and firing, eligibility for participation, and so on. But governance is important even to the family's goal of mentoring the next generation, by establishing the structure that will define the steps needed for assimilating new family members.

Typically, when families look at the situations that require structure, they get stuck in the emotional webs of one of three common governance crises:

1) When sibling rivalry provokes one party into refusing to participate in a family enterprise.

2) When a sibling needs to be fired.

3) Management of common property.

Surviving a Family Crisis

Real life doesn't always follow the family's written mission statement, and for family members operating a business together, a level playing field can quickly turn into a slippery slope. Heightened levels of emotion caused by sibling rivalry and the specter of adolescent petulance linger like the flu and rage into full-blown fever when the family is caught off-guard by the death of the founder.

When Theresa Lawrence's (not her real name) father, the founder of an international business, died nearly two decades ago, the family began a series of dramatic shifts. With the patriarch gone, the family required a new governance structure, and critical decisions about the business needed to be made by the survivors—the founder's wife and children.

The family decided they would sell the business a year after their father's death. Although Lawrence says this decision was easy because none of them had the technical expertise to keep the business going, subsequent issues nearly divided the family, and in fact did cause a rift between two of the siblings. The family had established a procedure for managing the liquidity from the sale and the completion of the pending contracts from the engineering business. The second generation started another company, which they still operate and which is headed by Lawrence, the eldest daughter. Theresa Lawrence spent many years in investment banking and had the business expertise and the desire to lead the company. The first few years after the sale of their father's business were rocky ones for the family. "We'd had an awful lot of emotional trauma," says Lawrence, not least of which were the actions of her brother, Bill. He decided that he did not want to proceed with his mother and siblings, but was bound by the buy-sell agreement to wait a few years before the rest of the family could purchase his share. He soon stopped attending family board meetings.

Lawrence says Bill had long-simmering resentments about his place in the family and his perception of his father's treatment of him. "Part of it was that my father was imposing, and my brother never felt he could measure up," says Lawrence. Combined with the fact that Lawrence's father had mentored her husband, who was working in the family business, Bill felt he had been unfairly treated. To add further insult, in her brother's eyes, in 1989 their mother set up trusts to equalize the holdings among the grandchildren. "He was angry that she didn't talk to him beforehand. I was named as co-trustee with each of the parents because we were [classified as a Subchapter S company] and our accountants believed we needed central control of the paperwork. He wanted his wife as co-trustee." When he confronted his mother, she blamed Lawrence, and he consequently transferred his anger to his sister, but didn't tell her. "I didn't know until a year later when I wanted to visit him and he wouldn't let me come," says Lawrence. "After the rift, it got worse and worse over time. It wasn't just one event," says Lawrence. "At first, when he signed the buy-sell agreement, he stopped coming to shareholder meetings." According to Lawrence, the situation was so bad that "he felt my mother was taking sides when she would sit with my husband and me at lunch."

According to Lee Hausner, "Everyone has a gunnysack that we fill with personal trauma. As the sack fills, you can't continue to keep it under lock and key." In situations like Lawrence's, the resentment her brother was stuffing into his sack eventually boiled over and he felt he had to cut himself off from the family. Hausner says that the situation was exacerbated by the fact that one sibling (Lawrence) became a quasiparent when she was named cotrustee of the other trusts. The only way that action could have been successful, says Hausner, is if Lawrence's mother had explained to each of her children ahead of time how she planned to handle the trusts and each sibling had agreed to the plan. "Otherwise, all the backlog of sibling rivalry and competition blows out right then," she says.

"When families work together, they must have ongoing meetings or people will sit on their anger and hostility." Hausner adds, "If you don't express it, it's your fault. Nobody's a mind reader." Regular meetings of the family council will help families anticipate scenarios and practice their communication skills for when they need them the most.

It's not unusual for family aggression to spill over following the death of a parent. Hausner says, "Every generation has to build its own sense of how to connect. If they are already connected (before the loss of a parent) then it's because they choose to be, not because they are forced into it." Just as her father's death accentuated the family problems, the recent death of Lawrence's mother began the mending process. Since their mother's funeral, Lawrence's brother has made his first tentative steps back into the family some fifteen years after the initial rift. "I've read a lot about sibling rivalry and how the death of a parent either creates further dissension or a coming together because everyone grieves in a different way," says Lawrence. "The challenge is getting the family to come together. My brother recognizes that it's hard for him to forgive," she says. Her link with him now is still somewhat strained. "I'm not around him very much, but we have an e-mail relationship. Certainly it's much more cordial and he wrote in a recent e-mail that he wishes the last ten to fifteen years had been different."

At their mother's funeral, Lawrence's children and her brother's children met for the first time since they were toddlers. Now between the ages of 17 and 20, Lawrence says, "I don't know if they will keep in touch," although her son invited his cousin to join him at Vail over winter break. "All I'm looking for is a respectful and cordial relationship. I'm looking for Bill to want to be in the same room with me."

This family eventually solved it governance dilemma by allowing for the fact that not every past hurt or resentment can be overcome and sometimes a little time and distance help. By acting quickly to dissolve the business relationship with the disgruntled sibling, the rest of the family was free to move the business forward according to their common values and mission. Experts counsel that not every family can expect to remain a solid unit through each situation, but in the case of the Lawrence family, peeling off one member who wanted to go in his own direction did not harm the clan because the remaining siblings made the effort to continue on.

Although they experienced pain in the process, the pull of being a family is slowly bringing the Lawrences back together again. In the meantime, the business thrived with the commitment of the rest of the family, who have also been active in mentoring the next generation in both their philanthropic efforts and in the family business.

Even with a common set of values and a stated mission, families sometimes can't prevent one member from splintering off if he feels he's been mistreated. After all, until a crisis occurs, the family doesn't really have the opportunity to test its mission. When problems do erupt, it will help the family to regroup around its common values and reiterate the mission. If that doesn't work, perhaps the mission needs to change to reflect the changed circumstances and new challenges.

Removal Process

As often as a member of the second generation decides to extricate himself from the family, there are just as many times when the family must remove an unproductive member from its business or foundation. "This is the most painful thing families have to do," says Gerald Le Van. "There is a strong inclination to ignore, deny, or defer decisions on family underperformance. Or to reverse decisions once made. Sometimes we see the same family member fired and rehired a half-dozen times."

In too many instances, says Le Van, the family businesses will hire the divorcing daughter who needs something to do or the down-sized son-in-law who is out of a job, but who may not be qualified for the positions they hold, says Le Van. Family "employers of last resort" who don't apply sensible entry rules may be creating unfortunate situations that will become exceedingly difficult and painful to resolve later.

Family businesses and foundations are wonderful places for family members to work together for the family's common vision, but if they are not motivated, they become a drag on the financial success and the morale of the family and the firm. As discussed in Chapter 1, family companies have to go through a progression and become professionalized if they are to survive to the third genera- tion. The same is true for a family foundation. Unproductive family employees have to perform or they must be let go.

When a family has to fire one of its own, it should be able to point to a policy as a guide, one that was developed by the family council. As we discussed in Chapter 1, if the unproductive family member is in the business, better to have oversight by a committee that includes the human resources director, the chairman of the board, and the CEO, along with several family members. The policy, whether it is for a family foundation or for a business, has to include reasonable entry rules for employment and periodic job performance reviews based on objective criteria. Training for the job should be spelled out and if the next generation is to begin at a young age, a coach and mentor should be provided to guide the development of the trainee. This will provide a shield for the family and if it is made public to family members up front, there will be little chance for argument if the ax has to come down.

According to Ivan Lansberg, the key to being able to remove an unproductive family employee is in the documentation. "Make sure a track record of unsatisfactory performance is gathered," he advises, and don't let hearsay from other family members be the determining factor. Even if the process is an objective one, the fired family member may not see it that way and may spiral into an angry destructive force focused against the family. That's why Lansberg counsels families not to forget that they are still a family and they need to have a plan of action already in place to deal with the fired relative. "The best of families go to extraordinary lengths to recycle the person and put them in a career path that is more compatible with their interests and talents," he says. "A lot of the time, after the initial pain, [the person] feels relief. Often they know they are not in alignment with the company and are failing."

Be generous in helping the fired individual find a new productive path, whether that path involves a sabbatical, further education,
career counseling, or even therapy. "You have to be honest with the
person, and then do the family work," says Lansberg. That family
work includes reinforcing the reality that family members will be
treated the same way that other employees are treated. Don't post-
pone, Lansberg counsels. "Detect and correct early. The longer you
wait, the harder it is on the family."

Dealing with Multiple Owners

Another aspect of working together as a family is managing inherited
lands and vacation homes. Once again, if the family doesn't treat the
venture in a professional manner, emotions may take over and stifle
the enjoyment of the property, or even force a sale that will promote
finger pointing and resentment.

The acquisition of the property usually begins with the lofti-
est intentions. Founders who are building a family's legacy seek a
retreat where they can gather with the family to recharge and create
memories for generations to come. What they often don't envision is
the complexity and future expense of managing the retreat once the
family expands into the third and fourth generations. If the home or
land becomes the focus of local developers, the pressure to sell can
divide cousins and siblings. If it is too small to accommodate more
than one family at a time, fights can erupt over who gets the Fourth
of July or the Labor Day weekend. Subsequent generations, just as
adamant about saving the cherished family memories, strive to preserve the founder's legacy, but often at a tremendous cost in terms
of collaboration and financial commitment.

The story of Monica Smith (not her real name) and her family is
far too typical. She has many fond memories of her time at the beach
house her father built. "It was a magical place," she says. Ironically,
in order to preserve the family harmony that was nourished during
vacations at that very same house, she had to divest herself of all
interest in it, both emotional and financial.

Smith, her sister, and her brother were given joint ownership in
the house after her father's death. While her father was alive, Smith

says, "everything went smoothly because he was in charge of it." After he died, however, her brother took control, despite the fact that the three siblings had equal shares in the property. Describing him as "impossible to deal with," Smith says her brother made unilateral decisions without informing the rest of the family, ultimately causing Smith and her sister to sell their shares to their mother.

Smith recalls, "I got a call from an attorney less than a year after my father's death. He told me that a contractor was threatening to sue us over remodeling at the beach house. I said, 'What contractor?'" Smith had no idea her brother had hired someone to work on the house. The lawyer informed Smith that the contractor was suing all three owners. "I said this is too risky for me to be in a situation where my brother and mother had power over me. It frightened me."

Smith's mother has since given her brother a 51 percent ownership stake in the house and will leave him the remaining share in her estate. "It was a great house," Smith says, "however, what I had to think about was my peace of mind. There's a point where your own peace of mind has a higher value, and with all the difficulty and strife, you lose the enjoyment of the property anyway."

Whenever families own an asset together, there is bound to be disagreement about its management—everything from who pays for repairs to who left wet towels on the couch. Add in the sentimentality that everyone associates with the property and the discussions become tainted with emotion.

"It's the little things that make it difficult for people to stay together in a family business," says Olivia Boyce-Abel, founder of Family Lands Consulting. "And make no mistake about it—when families share ownership of a home or land, they are in business together." Boyce-Abel speaks from her own personal experience, which inspired her to found Family Lands Consulting after years of conflict over her family's shared property.

Boyce-Abel says that families must communicate and set up a clear governance structure regarding how decisions will be made in order to succeed in common ownership. Often, the ownership structure was determined generations earlier, but as families grow, communication among all family members becomes a necessity in order to avoid nasty disagreements now and in the future.

In her own family, Boyce-Abel felt the lack of both communication and governance associated with an inherited tract of land. Her situation was exacerbated by having tenants in common ownership, a method frequently used by parents looking for a way to leave property equally to their heirs, but also a method that doesn't have a built-in decision-making structure.

Boyce-Abel's grandfather bought 3,000 acres of land along the South Carolina coast, which included one of the last undeveloped barrier islands on the east coast. His initial outlay, eighty years earlier, grew in value to millions of dollars by the time Boyce-Abel, her siblings, and their cousins were adults. "More important to me, it was a very special place," she says. "We went there every summer for most of my life." Problems with sharing ownership, however, were brewing in each generation.

Her grandfather's will left an undivided interest in the land (an arrangement whereby each person owns a percentage of the whole) to Boyce-Abel's mother, her uncle, and her grandmother. After the grandmother died, her third went into a trust for the grandchildren. Disagreement soon arose between Boyce-Abel's mother and uncle over the division of the inheritance. The will stipulated that the grandmother's share be divided equally among the grandchildren, which Boyce-Abel's uncle interpreted to mean 50 percent for his two children, and 50 percent for his sister's four children. Furthermore, her uncle wanted to develop the majority of the land into a resort, whereas her mother wanted to leave it in its natural state.

Boyce-Abel's mother desperately wanted to keep the entire tract of land preserved, but during estate tax planning realized her heirs wouldn't be able to afford the multimillion-dollar tax bill that would become due upon her death. Her solution was to create a tax-exempt 501(c)(3) and gift the land to that entity, qualifying it as a charitable donation. In addition, she sought to place a conservation easement on the land that would preclude much in the way of future development. That would lower the market value of the land, thus saving estate taxes and making it easier for her heirs to keep it intact. Although these two actions enabled Boyce-Abel's mother to meet her primary goals, she had paved the way for a series of legal battles involving the rest of the family, and the disagreement over the land and its use continued into the next generation, which included Boyce-Abel. Problems arose because her siblings didn't understand what their mother was doing, says Boyce-Abel, and two of them tried to overturn her will. "Her lifelong goal was to preserve the land in its entirety, and she tried to do that. The ownership was in a complicated structure," says Boyce-Abel. By the mid-1980s, the land was under multiple ownership that included her mother, her now late-uncle's wife, and through her late grandmother's trust, Boyce-Abel, her siblings, and her cousins. The trust meant Boyce-Abel and her generation did not owe estate taxes, but they had a low basis in the property.

The outcome of the family's miscommunication was played out in court. "We had five different lawsuits going," says Boyce-Abel. With respect to the feelings of her siblings concerning land conservation, "we settled by having my mother's share go to a local university for marine biology research, so her 1,000 acres were preserved." At the same time, Boyce-Abel's aunt and cousins went to court to ask a judge to partition the property. Seeking to devise their own solutions to estate planning in case of her aunt's death, "my cousins and aunt wanted to determine which piece of property was theirs," says Boyce-Abel. The judge partitioned the land and a third of it is preserved, as her mother had intended. "I still own a portion of the land through the trust," says Boyce-Abel, however her enjoyment in the property has been diminished by her experience in court. The fallout from the litigation for the family is that "we do not have the same family closeness. We have started the process of healing, but it's very difficult when you're on opposite sides of the courtroom."

There are so many challenges for siblings, cousins, and other relatives when sharing a common property that go beyond ownership, namely maintenance and use complexities. Ken Huggins, EdD, professor of English at Monroe Community College in Rochester, New York, wrote *How to Pass It On: The Ownership and Use of Summer Houses*, a companion piece to the book *Passing It On,* by his late sister, Judith Huggins Balfe. A sociologist by profession, Balfe had interviewed more than seventy families about passing on summer homes. Ken Huggins points to five common issues that impede families sharing a vacation home:

1) How the time periods are determined for each family member.

2) Who in the family serves as landlord, and does that person deserve special treatment with respect to preference on time slots or payment for her services?

3) How do family members qualify for their own time slot? When they marry? When they have children?

4) How is status gained in blended or divorced families? Does the divorced spouse of a blood relative lose time at the house with his children?

5) How does the home pass to the subsequent generations? Only through blood relatives? Or can others receive part of the ownership?

Even considering this list, Huggins notes that there are so many issues that parents don't anticipate. Generally, while founders are alive and still in control, the system works well. Parents dole out the time parcels and act as landlords. They continue to finance the home and maintain its upkeep. Once the second generation takes control, sibling rivalry often becomes exacerbated around the summer home, Huggins says.

"The next generation has a lot more people, who all want a slot during the prime summer months that work around the school schedule. It becomes very difficult to divide up the time." Move down another generation, and the situation intensifies. "In the third generation you're talking about cousins who don't have the same commitment that the siblings had, and don't even know each other as well. Now you have six to twelve family units all wanting to use the home during a couple of peak months."

He recommends that families develop a document, like a constitution, that will be used to resolve all questions about finance and management. For example, summer homes are often built on prime real estate that is escalating in value. Consequently, the costs of maintaining the home and the taxes are constantly rising. If a trust set up by the parents no longer pays these costs, the constitution will provide guidance as to when the family should consider selling the home.

The constitution will include an operating agreement that addresses maintenance costs, who pays for repairs, and how the costs are divvied up. For example, families need to decide if a sibling who earns more will pay more for upkeep, for a tradeoff of first dibs on the much-coveted July Fourth or Labor Day holidays. The more detailed the constitution and operating agreement, the more likely a family is to avoid arguments that can center on seemingly small details. "There's so much sentimental value attached to a house that you can't even throw out an old couch" without other siblings declaring that it was their favorite childhood piece of furniture, says Huggins.

Huggins recommends updating the constitution every five years, based on additions and relocations within the family. One sibling may move across the country and not want to share in ownership of a home that is rarely used. Huggins also recommends teaching children the value of the property and the financial cost of its upkeep. If children are kept in the dark by parents, they can't be expected to understand the ramifications of family decisions. Families who have a structured method for teaching the next generation assist their children in learning responsibility. Huggins wished he knew ahead of time the challenges he would face and he has tried to instill in his own children a sense of accountability.

Like Boyce-Abel, Huggins speaks from personal experience. His parents actually built two summer homes on adjoining lots in Nantucket. One home was for the parents and the other was for their four adult children to share with their growing families. The intent was for both homes to pass to the four children when their father died, with the eldest son having the right to buy out the ownership of the siblings' house and use the proceeds to support the maintenance of the parents' house. The four siblings would then own that home. Numerous problems arose after the father died,

in large part because he had neglected to discuss his plans with his
children. They were stunned and had many unanswered questions.
In addition, while their mother was alive, Huggins and his two
sisters felt that she favored the oldest son with the prime summer
slots. Resentment built among the siblings. When their mother died,
Huggins and his two sisters decided to buy their brother's interest in
the house they had shared and he, in turn, bought out their share in
the other. The arrangement worked well, Huggins says, because one
sister lived out west and hardly visited, leaving two siblings to share
one house, and their brother had use of the other.

Their solution laid to rest the immediate problems, but an
expensive one was looming. Their increasingly valuable property was
costing Huggins and his sisters a pretty penny, and eventually they
were forced to sell their house. Taxes were thousands of dollars in
the last year they owned the house, and it was costing nearly twice
that amount in yearly expenses. "My kids were very upset about selling and wanted to try renting, but we would have to rent the whole
summer to make enough to keep it, and we wouldn't ever get to use
it," he says.

Although it was hard for everyone to give up a home that had
provided so many good memories, Huggins claims that younger
generations should be prepared to face facts. He says teaching them
about the responsibilities of home ownership at a young age will
help prepare them for what the future might bring. "I never knew
while my parents were alive what was involved," and it might have
helped, Huggins says.

He suggests that parents start early to teach respect for the property. "Make sure kids understand it's not a free lunch. There's a cost
in terms of effort and finance," he says. "As young kids, have them
do things besides just having fun, whether it's gardening or some
other chore, so they're involved in the ownership of the house and
they understand there are responsibilities. When they are older, talk
to them about the cost of keeping up the place."

If the property remains in the family through another generation,
the children will understand the various challenges of management.
They can continue the operating agreement or establish a new one.

They will be able to convene the families and discuss maintenance and house rules and make sound and fair judgments regarding the property. If the property has to be sold, they will understand the decision even though they may feel the loss of a special place. When they become adults, they will have firsthand knowledge of the complications of property management and will be better equipped to make their own decisions about owning property.

Huggins points to various structures that founders can establish to preserve family homes and land, but cautions that it's wise to discuss each option with attorneys before making a decision. The options include trusts, partnerships, associations, corporations, and conservation easements.

Trusts may be an ideal way to provide income for upkeep and repairs, but Huggins says the downside of trusts is that if real estate values increase rapidly, the trust income may prove insufficient to cover costs. Trusts are also impersonal and may not take into account the changing needs of the family's future generations.

With partnerships, "one share, one vote" may sound equitable, but Huggins points out that when siblings have their own children, equality goes out the window. Partnerships might work for the second generation, but beyond that, they can become problematic and cumbersome if the number of partners increases too rapidly. However, partnerships provide an easy way for one party to buy out the other. Ultimately, Huggins believes, partnerships might make good financial sense, but they may not work when usage and maintenance issues come into play.

As unincorporated legal organizations with formal by-laws, associations can detail usage and maintenance. As owner of the property, the association can be sued for liability, but not the individual members. In addition, because individuals own multiple shares, it is possible to minimize inheritance tax.

More costly and complex than associations, corporations offer the benefits of associations. The drawbacks and benefits both come from the tax situation. In a Subchapter S corporation, shareholders receive profits, on which they pay taxes and are responsible for losses. In a C Corporation, the corporation itself receives the profits and losses and pays taxes at the outset. Remaining profits or losses are passed on to individuals, who will also have to pay taxes. Because corporations must hold annual shareholder meetings and elect officers, Huggins feels this is the "least-worst" option, especially for large families in second- or third-generation ownership.

Sometimes called a conservation restriction, an easement can benefit families who own land they want to pass along to heirs. The easements remove the possibility of one heir trying to cash out for the big bucks promised by developers. A legal agreement between the landowner and a land trust or government agency, the conservation easement limits the use of the land, with some flexibility for development and use, but the family retains ownership. For example, family members are able to plan for building sites for their own homes. If the land is farmed, those activities can still be conducted. Families can save estate taxes if the land is sold at a bargain rate or donated to a family foundation or some tax-exempt vehicle. One of the main benefits of the easement, says Boyce-Abel, is that "potential fights for selling the land for top dollar development go away. It's a wonderful tax planning and preservation tool."

The key to any of the governance crises is the strength of the family's mission, communication, and governance structures. Written guiding principles and operating missives will provide a foundation for family members when they find themselves at odds. If the structure or the mission weakens under pressure, families have to decide if it is because of one lone dissenter or if others are also unhappy, in which case, the structure needs revision.

Preparing the Next Generation

Mentoring is most effective when it involves the efforts of the entire family. As we saw in the previous chapter, mentoring the next generation seals the family's commitment to multigenerational wealth. Let's look at a variety of ways to do that.

Nurturing and guiding the up-and-coming family members is the natural next step for families who have established a council and governance of its various enterprises. Mentoring and teaching are often occurring at the same time in the family. For example, while instructing children on sound financial practices, families are also mentoring them by demonstrating their fiscal values and by nurturing their development through stages as they grow.

With the family mission statement as a guideline for values, the young members of the third or fourth generation gain knowledge about how the family operates as a unit. As they mature, they can be included as nonvoting members on the family board of directors or participate in the family's philanthropic initiatives, putting the mission statement into practice and beginning to learn how to work within a family unit.

A variety of excellent resources exist for teaching and guiding the next generation. Hap Perry, of Asset Management Advisors, has a curriculum for parents and children that begins with preschool and continues through young adulthood. There are games and books for parents and children to explore together, as well as extracurricular programs, such as trips to Wall Street and fiscal education camps where children spend time learning the basics of budgeting, saving, and investing. Asset Management Advisors also conducts sessions with families during which the young people role-play positions within the family foundation or business. They may act as board members, executives, or nonactive voting family members. The objective of these sessions is to teach children the family's governance procedures in a manner that they will understand and remember.

Family councils can develop their own educational and mentoring programs for the family based on the needs of its members and the next generation. In mature families with numerous enterprises, the council will determine a host of criteria for the participation of the next generation, including appropriate age, education level, inclusion of spouses, and more specific issues depending on the family's needs. Some of the specifics, such as policies concerning employment within the family business, have been discussed.

We will continue to explore ways to teach the next generation about wealth in Part III. Parents who are lax in their responsibility of guiding and mentoring the next generation will quickly see the consequences in the behavior of the heirs. Working together as a family means not only solving the immediate crises as they occur, but also developing the policies and procedures that will direct its multigenerational success.

In the next chapter, the dilemma facing wealthy families is specific to marriage and partnership. When one partner is much less wealthy than the other, both have to come to terms with the financial capital in order to move forward in the relationship, and ultimately have the right attitude about money to pass along to subsequent generations.

Chapter Five

Integrating New Family Members

THE DILEMMA:

As new members come into the clan through marriage, how do I level the playing field if one partner is less wealthy, and what value do certain structures like prenuptial agreements offer me?

UNEQUAL WEALTH can be the cause of great discomfort in a relationship, as damaging labels of gold digger, trophy wife, and sugar daddy are gleefully whispered in polite society whenever one of their own marries someone of lesser means. Compounding the situation, if the wealthier partner hasn't come to grips with the family fortune, it becomes nearly impossible to create a union in which each partner feels on equal footing, much less united to the extent they can mentor the next generation. Caught in their own cycle of self-destruction, they begin to fracture the family often without realizing the lessons of dysfunction they are teaching the younger generation.

Tension is created because while the wealth of one partner can enable the new couple to begin writing a family narrative together, the unspoken implication is that the one with the money has the right to more privileges and a greater say in how the couple's wealth is spent. In other words, the wealthier person has more power in the relationship. Equalizing the power comes only when couples reach a mutual understanding about the wealth.

As the couple is reaching accord, both partners must be attentive to the perceptions and concerns of other family members, who are sometimes threatened by a new marriage if the wealth has been in the nuclear family until that point. Parents of the betrothed worry that the family's fortune or business may be lost if the couple divorces in the future. Children from a previous marriage worry that their portion of the wealth will be diverted through estate planning if the new spouse is given a large portion or income from a trust meant for them.

Various solutions (prenuptial agreements being the most common) can provide comfort to the new spouse as well as to the rest of the family. But first, couples need to work out their different philosophies about money. In this chapter, we will consider the following issues:

- *Understanding emotions concerning money:* Gender differences play an important role in the attitude toward wealth.
- *Easing discomfort:* Various methods help partners level the playing field with regard to the estate and their relationship to it.
- *Considering a contract:* Prenuptial agreements are among the most popular and effective solutions for many couples.

Few topics in a relationship are more vexing than sex and money. Often, when couples sit down to talk about either topic, it's the discussion about money that, with reference to Sir Winston Churchill, becomes "a riddle wrapped in a mystery inside an enigma." When one partner has significantly more wealth than the other, issues of self-esteem and expectations about who should be the breadwinner further distort the discussion. Also complicating the situation are issues of gender. Men and women think differently about finance and understanding these deep-seated beliefs will help couples see why their partner behaves in a certain way when it comes to writing a check for a vacation or buying a house.

It also makes a difference whether the money is earned or

received by way of an inheritance. As we'll learn in Part III, inheritors have money issues of their own, one of which is that they really don't feel they own the money unless they've earned it. It's a double whammy—inheritors who are uncomfortable with their wealth and also hold the purse strings—and it doesn't bode well for the relationship.

Understanding Emotions Concerning Money

Gender differences play an important role in one's attitude toward wealth, as Jane Newman (not her real name) learned. Her wealth, achieved through inheritance, was a cloud over both her marriages, although she finally discovered a workable solution in her second marriage. Newman, 64, has been married to her second husband for twenty-five years, but notes that initially she failed to avoid the same financial pitfalls she had encountered during her first marriage.

As an heiress, Newman struggled emotionally throughout her younger years with the fact that she received a check regularly from her trustee, but had no job at the time. She met her first husband in graduate school, where he earned a doctoral degree and a teaching position. They were both 23 when they married. As a young adult, Newman attempted to hide her wealth from her friends and tried not to rely on it. So, what her husband did next was a surprise.

As Newman tells the story, "After two years of work, he wanted to quit to become a writer. I felt uneasy about that, but didn't say anything. We had a baby and moved to Berkeley, California, and he wrote some poetry." Her husband had no intention, however, of being a *poete maudit*. "Looking back," Newman says, "he made a choice to live off my income, though we had never discussed it." Newman admits there were other problems in the marriage and eventually he left her for another woman.

Newman was not at ease with her role as financial controller in the relationship. Seven years later, she met and married her second husband. Although she says she tried to avoid being the main source of income again, "It happened anyway, but for different reasons." She says that her husband is very bright, but "has a low tolerance for stress." She insisted that he work and he hated it. He became so stressed, Newman says, "I suggested he stop for a while, and for him that meant never going back." That was about sixteen years ago. "For years after that, we went to a therapist and I raised this issue repeatedly. It took me years, but I've come to accept it."

Reflecting on the situation, Newman thinks her own work ethic was causing her to feel as though her husband had failed her. By this time, she was working and "also believed that the man should work." Compounding the problem, Newman says, was that "his income, while he was working, was actually much lower than mine. I think that also makes a difference. There's such a connection in our society between worthiness and income. Americans have been taught to value work by how much money can be made."

She has come to accept her situation because of the financial bargain they've struck. When her husband was working, he presented her with monthly accounts of what he had spent, and asked her to pay him half that amount, because his income didn't cover the expenses. "It was somewhat like coming cap in hand," Newman says. Then she hit on an idea "that blew our minds. I could split my income with him." For the past nine years, Newman has been sharing her net income with her husband and says, "I don't think he feels any shame in that."

Well before a financially unequal relationship becomes serious, the couple should discuss how each partner feels about the unequal wealth. That will provide the basis for moving forward. According to Jay Hughes, "the most critical thing in my study of this [issue] is that you have to have discussions about the hard question, and the hard question is not how *much* money, but what is your philosophy about money?" Fiscally unequal partnerships can work if couples disclose their expectations about money and then take the steps necessary to make them both feel they're on equal footing, whether those steps involve prenuptial agreements, annual gifting programs, or equalizing assets during estate planning. The key is that the couple has common understanding before committing to a structure.

Hughes has had the opportunity to practice what he preaches. He is in a relationship with an heiress, Jackie Merrill, who has considerably more wealth than he has. Merrill, a third generation member of a wealthy family, knows whereof she speaks on the issue of unequal wealth because of her past marriage, her relationship with Hughes, and as founder and president of CenterPoint, which offers a program of facilitated discussions in creative self-expression. According to Merrill, "the most important thing is to develop consciousness about what money and control mean. The biggest hazard is to go merrily along and it's like an elephant in the room that is invisible and unrecognized."

Feeding the dilemma of unequal wealth, however, are gender differences. It seems the old maxim about men choosing women for their youth and appearance and women choosing men for their ability to provide money and security still holds true. When the man has more money in a relationship, Hughes says, "from a sociological standpoint and cultural standpoint, that is the norm. If you look at the general distribution of wealth in societies, you would see that, historically and currently, men have more." Women want men to bring wealth into a relationship for their security and that of their children. While Hughes was a practicing attorney in trusts and estates, he says that he commonly detected opposite behaviors between men and women, namely the capacity for men to willingly make (monetary) gifts to women, and the reverse situation of women not making gifts to men. As an example, he describes a couple entering a first marriage, where the man has net worth of $5 million and the woman has $100,000. In estate planning discussions, Hughes would recommend that the husband build the wife's estate, at least to the credit shelter amount in order to save on estate taxes. "He'll say, 'oh fine, how do I do that?' and it's over. 'I love her, it's fine, what difference does it make?'" Hughes points out that "underlying this [attitude] is the very deep male awareness that he can make the money again." Hughes adds that, on the flip side, if he were to make the same recommendation to the woman as the wealthier partner, she would be reluctant. "She thinks, 'I'm supposed to get resources from the man and I have no expectation that I could make [the wealth] again.'" The woman, Hughes says, would declare that she was uncomfortable with equalizing the estate, if in fact the man hadn't already said

"I don't need this." Hughes further notes that many women would not give their husbands the annual gift exclusion amount allowed by federal law in order to lessen their eventual estate taxes, "even when happily doing that for their children and grandchildren. They would give him a nice tie."

At the root of this gut reaction, Hughes says, is the often-cited bag-lady syndrome. "Women over the age of 70 whom I've represented always felt they didn't have enough cash, even if they had hundreds of millions. I think this gets right at the heart of this fiscal inequality." Women are basically more insecure than men when it comes to making and keeping money. "This is not pop science. This is evolutionary science, and whether we like it or not, it's real."

Hughes boils it down this way: In many of his academic writings, psychologist Carl Jung cited the need for men in their early 20s to early 40s to find meaningful work as a calling and then integrating their female side when they focus on relationships. Conversely, women will be working on their relationship side in early adulthood, to be followed by a more masculine side in finding work as a calling in their second stage of life. How men and women make the passages through these critical points in their development, separately and as a couple, will tell whether they crash and burn or persevere. "Men and women who understand their Jungian roles can really get insight into their psyches," Hughes says. As Jung himself stated, "Where love rules, there is no will to power and where power predominates, there love is lacking. The one is the shadow of the other."

As an example of Jung's theory in financially unequal partnerships, Hughes describes a woman, who in her younger years, "turns to the man in her life and says 'please take care of all my financial affairs.' Then at 50 (when she finds work as a calling) she wants to take it back." If her husband's place in life is built around being her money manager, and he's also in the process of getting in touch with his female (relationship-building) side, "it all crashes horribly. We see this all the time."

Hughes and Merrill agree that the age at which they met was critical. He was 49 and she was 52 and they've been together for twelve years. "There are forces at work at different stages in people's lives, whether wealth is involved or not," says Merrill. She has noticed more discomfort, particularly in women who have more wealth than their partners, during the younger years. "There is tremendous self-consciousness and discomfort among women in their 20s and 30s that tends to neutralize the older they get," says Merrill. "It's a very tender issue in the 20s and 30s, which is when most of these women are getting married." During a conference where she was a featured speaker, Merrill recalls a wealthy young woman who said that she was afraid to have her husband's boss over for dinner, because she and her husband lived in a grander style than he did.

In her younger years, Merrill says she had her own self-exploration to do before she was comfortable in a partnership of fiscal inequality. Her parents had given her messages about her wealth that she later felt she had to overcome, and did so with the help of a psychotherapist. "We looked at the stuck places in my own psyche that didn't allow me to be free from the messages of upbringing or culture." Her father had said that a marriage in which the woman had more money would never work and Merrill recalls that in her first two marriages, "I proceeded to play that out." Her mother, who never had any money of her own, told Merrill that she should keep her money for herself. Therefore, her first two entrepreneurial husbands received none of her wealth. "I didn't even consider the merits of investing in their business," she says. "I realized I had this insidious tape in my head that even though I had more money, the man was supposed to take care of me." She says couples need to look beyond cultural stereotyping and ask, "Are we going along with what's been imprinted in our minds or are we making our own way, free to choose our own views?"

Couples don't have to go it alone. Merrill says she is "a huge fan" of premarital counseling and she advises couples to choose a counselor who has experience with fiscal inequality in relationships. Specifically, she recommends asking if the counselor was ever in a fiscally unequal relationship and what experience he or she has had with these types of clients. Also ask for referrals, she says. Most people find counselors through recommendations from friends or relatives.

Easing Discomfort

Various methods help partners even things out with regard to the estate and their relationship to it. When couples hash out their financial philosophies about money, it becomes a relatively easy asset to divvy up in accordance with their mutual agreement. The gesture from the wealthier partner will signal a willingness to put the money behind them so they can work on the other issues that will inevitably crop up in a relationship.

Placing the less wealthy partner on firm financial footing also enables that person to feel equal on other fronts. With all the prevailing associations of money and power, it is best if one partner doesn't feel the need to go to the other begging for every expense. If that happens, the feeling of being trivialized will eventually overpower the relationship.

Merrill says couples don't have to mathematically equalize estates, but the wealthier partner should provide the other with enough to promote a feeling of independence. She cites an example using what she terms "an enlightened family." Merrill tells of a wealthy family who had sons and were concerned that their daughters-in-law to be would hang on to a bad marriage for financial reasons. So at the time of the marriages, they gifted them money so the daughters-in-law would never feel imprisoned in the marriage.

In another situation, one of Merrill's heiress friends married a teacher whose family placed a high priority on education. "Money was not valued in his family, so his wife's wealth meant nothing to him." His wife gifted money to him anyway. "It's important because it takes the element of dependency out of the relationship."

The measure of the man, however, is often how well he is able to accept a gift of money from his wife. "I'm sure some men hear implied messages about her money or her family's money," says Merrill, and it takes thoughtful examination on the part of both partners to be successful. "If a man is resentful of being gifted money, then they both have to look at the hidden dynamic between them so she can give freely, meaning that neither she nor her family can manage the money unless he wants it that way. If she's judging how he's spending it, then they will have problems."

For her part, Jane Newman doesn't have a formal contract requiring her to share her income with her husband. It's an informal arrangement that they've worked out through her money manager. "I could change it at any time," she says. "I could cut him off." The pact works for them and she says that "the older I get, the less I worry about it."

However when couples examine such structures as prenuptial and postnuptial contracts, estate equalization strategies, and even informal agreements, they need to be sure that form follows function. In other words, as Hughes cautions, uncover the function first and then find the form to fit. Too many of his legal colleagues, he notes, slap a form on the table without urging the couple to go through the emotional work of discovering their philosophies about money and its effect on the relationship. The result is that the form ultimately won't work because the couple hasn't done the work to reveal which aspects of their philosophies need adjustment.

Any solution a couple devises, as Jane Newman discovered, has to fit the needs of both partners. Though hers was worked out through trial and error, it still meets her and her husband's needs. If one partner comes to a conclusion on his own, however, and presents it to the other, though it might sound like a fix, it ultimately won't hold. This is especially true when the solution is a last-ditch effort and the couple didn't start with a discussion about their financial philosophies. Such was the case with Ray Potter (not his real name), the retired executive of a multinational company, who is trying to get his marriage back on track with a postnuptial agreement that he hoped would make his wife financially comfortable.

Potter married his significantly younger second wife with the expectation that his wealth would not become an issue. "I tried very hard to not make it a big part of the marriage," he says. He is now barely sidestepping divorce and blames their *crise de coeur* on financial difficulties, compounded by a difference in age. Potter had earned the good life. His stock options were flying high, and he and his wife lived accordingly. Their lavish existence plummeted in concert with the marriage when Potter's investments took a dive. Potter had borrowed on the stock options and is currently paying down the loan. After his wife filed for divorce, Potter convinced her that they should remain married for financial reasons. Most of their assets were tied up in the leveraged low-cost-basis stock and two low-tax-basis homes. If they had to sell the assets to pay off debt, "I realized we would each have less income and fewer assets," Potter says.

Potter reflects that in the beginning of the marriage, "when the price of the stock was going up, we started off the marriage with an annual budget. That quickly turned into an estimated cash flow." In order to make his wife feel at ease in their fiscal relationship, Potter gave her the freedom to spend as she liked and she chose to come to him if it were a significant amount, though he hadn't set a limit. "At one point, I had been giving her fairly expensive jewelry as gifts. There was a piece of jewelry, costing maybe $600 or $900, and she came to me and said 'I'd like this,' and I said, 'that's fine.' So she had a break point of what amount to talk to me about, and it worked pretty well."

Potter adds that he took that stance with his wife on purpose. "I wanted her to have a feeling of freedom. I tried not to use the unevenness of our wealth as a whip." Potter says he observed many of his wealthy friends placing their wives on a budget, but he rejected that idea. He further tried to alleviate any discomfort on his wife's part in his estate planning. He has four children from his first marriage and was contributing an annual gift of stock from his previous company into trusts for them. Because his wife is roughly the same age as his children, he also established a trust for her that would be set up through his will. He says he provided "a comfortable life." In addition to income from the trust, she would have the power to tap into the trust "for damn near anything."

During his estate planning, Potter says he avoided backlash from his children by discussing his plans with them. "They have their own lives and the trusts I established for them will provide a modest retirement. I've been fairly consistent in my discussions with them, emphasizing that healthy adults ought to be able to take care of themselves." He also sent them a copy of the postnuptial agreement he drafted with his wife.

Potter says now that he should have insisted on a prenup. He didn't have one in his first marriage, but he wasn't wealthy then. He built up his assets after his divorce from his first wife. "What I wanted to do with a prenup before my second marriage was take the money arguments out of the marriage," Potter says. "I wanted to be sure she was taken care of." When confronted with the prenuptial agreement, however, his second wife refused to sign and Potter dropped the discussion. "I got married because I was in love, not because I thought I would get a divorce."

The postnuptial was a gesture that came too late in the marriage. Once the die was cast, it was hard for the couple to overcome the relationship roles they had taken on. As the wealthier partner, Potter had control even though he didn't hold his wife to a budget. As he himself has stated, a prenup written before the marriage might have put them on more solid footing. It is sometimes easier for the wealthier partner to gloss over or not realize the depth of the inequality because he has the power. It is incumbent on both partners to set in motion the communication and eventually the solution.

Potter did do something right—he communicated frequently with his children about his estate plans, so there was no misunderstanding that could tear apart the family. By providing copies of his postnuptial to his children, he signified his trust in them and his willingness to be open to questions. Although he may not save his marriage, he will have protected his relationship with his children.

When partners talk about money, they may be speaking from their own perspective, but the key is to see it from the other person's viewpoint and in some cases, change deeply ingrained assumptions. Both parties have to value what the less wealthy partner brings to the relationship. As Merrill says, "They both have to look beyond the man as breadwinner." To help couples get beyond the money, in her sessions Merrill asks each partner to develop a personal mission statement and then asks the couple to do the same. "It gets them on the higher ground," she says, "where the process is far more important than the outcome." The purpose of this exercise is to relegate money to its proper place and reveal the passions and values of each partner as an individual and as a couple. "Money can blur the real issues and become the arena for discussion, when in fact the discussion of values and goals may be masked." Merrill knows firsthand that it's not easy "to go deep and look inside. It's not something we're equipped to do on a daily basis." And both spouses have to be committed to working through it. Merrill continues, "I cannot underestimate the importance of choosing a great partner. With Jay (Hughes), I feel safe, and for the first time in a relationship, I revealed the extent of my net worth." Hughes spent a career as a trusts and estates attorney, and is still an active author and speaker. "His income far exceeds mine," Merrill allows. "It's not as if he's unproductive," she adds. "Jay is an unusual man and he's been dealing with these issues professionally for a long time. I'm very comfortable giving him gifts of money," she says. "I've come a long way."

There are many ways to be productive, not all of them financially rewarding; and certainly there are very few paths to earning the kind of wealth that is multigenerational. When one partner is overwhelmingly wealthy, the other partner will never be able to measure up fiscally and must be emotionally and intellectually strong enough to understand that what he or she is doing is still valuable. The wealthy partner's emotional support for this type of productivity puts the couple on level ground and leads both of them to expand their ideas of success.

When couples understand the importance each brings to the relationship, and have worked out their money philosophies, they inspire confidence in the rest of the family. Parents of the couple, who may have created the wealth, feel more comfortable about passing it along if they see that the union is strong and the money is kept in proper perspective. Children of the couple, who fear being left out, should be brought into the planning, and by observing what the parents have accomplished they are being mentored in a loving solid relationship. Even if parents don't share their estate-planning strategies to the degree that Ray Potter did, they still communicate their attitudes about money through their words and actions.

Considering a Contract

Passion and prudence are sometimes odd bedfellows in relationships. Prenuptial agreements, however, while arguably considered the cold shower of romance, can do more than prevent couples from engaging in the mutual *j'accuse* of a future divorce. They can also provide a forum for disclosure at the outset of a relationship, when it's important to clarify matters of the heart as well as of the wallet.

Hashing out the financial expectations and responsibilities before entering into marriage is not a recent trend. Indeed, throughout history, marriage contracts were commonplace in many cultures, and still are. Evidence of marriage contracts has been unearthed by archaeologists sifting through the remains of civilizations, from the ancient Egyptians to Elizabethan Londoners. In fact, a marriage contract dating from the seventh century BC was found wrapped around a mummified crocodile, the crocodile considered to be an offering to the gods. Prenups have a long history and remain one of the most popular contracts for couples looking to equalize their estates.

Most attorneys agree that virtually everyone would benefit from a prenuptial agreement, in terms of protecting current assets as well as future or anticipated wealth. Although detractors contend that prenuptial agreements kill romance, Arlene Dubin, author of *Prenups For Lovers* and a partner with the law firm of Sonnenschein Nath & Rosenthal LLP, says couples should at least consider one. Even if they ultimately don't draft the document, they've educated each other about their finances, she says. "Most people have some issues to cover," she adds, such as "closely held businesses, the intergenerational transfer of wealth, debts, or a wife who plans to leave the workplace to care for the children."

There are no statistics on the number of prenups drafted annually, but according to the American Academy of Matrimonial Lawyers, there is an increase in the number of wedded couples with prenups in place. Attorneys say that reasons vary, but include a national divorce rate of nearly 50 percent, a remarriage rate of 40 percent, and longer life expectancy. The baby-boomer generation has also amassed more wealth than its predecessors, meaning there is potentially more to lose in a divorce.

In addition, "more and more couples are marrying later, are more independent, and have accumulated more assets," says attorney Lisa A. Schneider, a partner at Gunster, Yoakley & Stewart in West Palm Beach, Florida. Those entering second or later marriages also want to protect their children's share of the accumulated wealth. "Anytime you have children from a previous marriage, you need a prenup or a plan for how your assets will pass," says Schneider.

"I'm doing them for grandparents (who are remarrying), who maybe in the past wouldn't have considered one," says Ken Edelman, an attorney specializing in estate planning in Boca Raton, Florida. He adds that he has also fielded requests from children concerned about parents who are remarrying, as well as from parents who plan to transfer wealth to their children and are anxious to protect the wealth.

Talking about money in the context of a relationship breaking up is not easy, and to some it feels like a negative cloud over the pending celebration of marriage. However, time won't ease the discomfort, and when prospective partners know right off the bat how the wealthy partner feels, it will be less awkward. "Prenups should be contemplated well before marriage and addressed like any other business issue, just like insurance and investments," says Schneider.

Couples usually find that discussing prenups can be thorny, yet difficulty in talking about important matters before marriage can be an omen of things to come. "If you have trouble communicating about prenups, you'll probably have trouble all the way through the marriage," says Chris Klein (not his real name). Klein, a wealthy entrepreneur, recently remarried and feels strongly about reaching a financial accord before the walk down the aisle. "Life will give you challenges," he says, but clarifying expectations around money will help solidify the relationship and prepare couples to meet those challenges. Schneider agrees. "If you're entering a marriage, I would hope you can reach conclusions about your joint and separate financial future. If it can't be done, maybe that's an indication of the [lack of] strength in the relationship."

To ease into the conversation about prenups, Dubin suggests that couples choose a neutral environment where both parties feel comfortable. Put all issues on the table, including careers, work schedules, sharing of household and childrearing duties, as well as all forms of income, debts, anticipated inheritance, trusts, and family business interests. Full disclosure is important. If one party intentionally omits financial information when a prenup is drafted, the document probably won't hold up in court.

Couples will need some breathing space to digest the information presented and to give more thought to their expectations. Don't force the communication and never sign a contract under duress. Instead, set aside five or six months before the wedding to work through the agreement, which still leaves time to experience the joy of planning the wedding.

Although some couples feel that the most difficult element of a prenup is broaching the subject to their intended spouse, often the initial communication is only the first hurdle. Depending on the complexity of the agreement, the two to four months it takes to negotiate and draft the document can be just as trying on a relationship.

When Jack King (not his real name), the wealthier partner in his marriage, describes the courtroom scene of a nasty divorce, he doesn't soften the image: "You and your spouse each hire a gladiator, and it's literally like being in the Coliseum in Rome, and your gladiator is trying to kill the other gladiator." King drafted a prenuptial agreement with his new wife to ensure that all financial obligations and roles were clearly understood before they recited their marriage vows. He says that during the process, they gained a deeper understanding of each other's goals and values. "Prenups are a great early warning indicator of how you'll deal with issues in a marriage," he notes. King speaks from the benefit of experience. He did not have a prenup in either his first or second marriages.

Charles Carson (not his real name), another wealthy entrepreneur who recently remarried, says his experience negotiating the prenup was tough, but worth it in the end. Although he says that he and his fiancée had "total compatibility, which made it easy to put our lives together," they found the process of drafting the contract painful at times because of disagreements over details. They agreed as a couple that she would leave a lucrative job to spend more time with him and they both wanted her to feel financially compensated for that decision.

Both men say their relationships are stronger now because they reached accord over the financial aspects of their marriage before they tied the knot. Both are just as adamant about not getting married without a prenup, no matter how difficult the journey. "Personally, I wouldn't leave home without it," says King.

Attorneys find that it's not only betrothed couples and those marrying for the second time who are considering prenups. Parents often have concerns about how marriage might affect the wealth they plan to transfer to the next generation or their children's share of a family-owned business.

When Carol and John Bird (not their real names) approached their two children about prenups, the initial reaction was predictably negative. The family had earned its wealth from a business they built and later sold. They had trusts set up for their children and planned to pass along some of their fortune. They wanted to protect their children's future wealth. Their son, Sam, who is 21, confides that he was initially against the idea of prenups. "Just the word *prenup* has a stigma," he says. Now that he has had further discussions with his family and their wealth advisers, he understands that the contracts are "a means to discuss how certain things, like debt or trusts, will be managed." Sam Bird is not currently in a serious relationship and he acknowledges that it will be awkward to talk about a prenup when the time comes. He plans to have further discussions with his parents and their advisers before broaching the topic. "It has to be done right," he says.

Carol and John Bird have had several conversations with their children about the benefits of prenups and they brought in outside counsel to help them. By explaining the benefits of prenups point by point, they were able to convince their children to at least consider them. Further discussion with the consultant was needed before the family could also come up with ways to broach the subject in a relationship. The consultant advised the children to raise the subject as soon as they thought the relationship was becoming serious and to be straightforward about it. Then allow the person time to absorb the information and ask some questions. It won't be accomplished in one discussion, but be open to further communication, the consultant suggested. One final but critical piece of advice: This is an area where parents have to allow the children to discuss prenups in their own way. They should not take part in discussions, but instead let the children learn to talk about the hard stuff and work through relationship difficulties themselves.

The most vocal proponents of prenups are typically those who have been through a divorce. They point out that the tendency to be more generous with money and property comes at the beginning of the relationship when both parties are eager to please the other. During a divorce battle, the gloves come off. Moreover, as both King and Carson know, the cost of a contested divorce can be high. If enough assets are at stake, and there is an impasse between the two parties, it can be catastrophic. The battle can last for years, and leave both sides emotionally and financially drained. As King says, "When one side's gladiator gets killed, they come up in the stands looking for your wallet." Having lost much, emotionally as well as financially, in his first divorce, he now wants his financial commitment to his new wife to be ironclad. "The emotional price of drafting a prenup is small compared to the emotional cost of a divorce," he says.

On the other hand, opponents of prenups argue that the agreements elevate money above people. At the happiest time in a couple's life, discussions revolve around a financial rather than an emotional commitment. The very mention of the word prenup also has the potential to explode the relationship. But King says that in his opinion, complications should be discussed before marriage. "Life will give you challenges, whether they involve kids or work or money," he says. Better to address those you know about before making the trip down the aisle.

Couples need to decide for themselves whether a prenup is the answer and not let the complexities of the contracts be the determining factor. If it is the right solution, then the difficulties will be a distant memory once the contract is drafted. After a couple agrees to the idea of a prenuptial agreement, there are factors to consider even before contacting an attorney, and couples should be fully aware of all the details. First and foremost is that the contracts require full disclosure of all assets and debts. In order for prenups to hold up in court, it's essential that the couple understands the nature of the other person's assets and debts, including business interests, trusts, insurance contracts, real estate holdings, collectibles, and future earning possibilities (for example, royalties from books or patents or an anticipated inheritance). Attorneys will usually attach an accounting of assets and debts to the contract.

To ensure against a future claim of coercion, each party should hire individual counsel. Case in point: movie director Steven Spielberg's first wife, actress Amy Irving, successfully fought the terms of her prenup because she reportedly was not represented by separate counsel when she signed the handwritten contract. Prenuptial agreements are binding contracts, and have the additional endorsement of the National Conference of Commissioners on Uniform State Laws. The commissioners, a group of attorneys, provide states with nonpartisan recommendations. The Uniform Premarital Agreement Act (UPAA), drafted in 1983, consists of guidelines regarding prenuptial agreements. Most states have adopted either this act or something similar.

Only the law and the court's determination of fairness limit the flexibility of a prenuptial agreement. For example, a person can't leave a spouse to fend for herself on welfare in the event of a divorce or forego child support, which is dictated by the courts. Obviously, prenups cannot support any illegal activity nor can they bypass an individual state's public policy laws, which vary from state to state. In some places, for example, it is against public policy for a prenuptial contract to prohibit a wife from becoming pregnant or to insist that she have an abortion if she does become pregnant, according to Dubin. The value of prenups is in the opportunity to override or rewrite law with regard to division of property. "When people are getting married, they are saying 'I do' to state laws," she adds. A prenuptial agreement allows couples to recognize what those laws are, and then to pick and choose, or modify, those statutes that would apply to their personal circumstance.

This is important because state laws vary when determining ownership of property by married couples. Nine states (Arizona, California, Idaho, Louisiana, Nevada, New Mexico, Texas, Washington, and Wisconsin) in the U.S. have community property laws, meaning that if there is a divorce, property is usually designated as belonging equally to both parties. In the other forty-one states, an equitable distribution system applies. Property is divided according to a variety of factors determined by a judge. The factors may include length of marriage, age of the partners, potential earning power, and whether there are children to be considered. In addition, some states have elective share or automatic spousal benefits. In Florida and New York, for example, spouses are generally entitled to one-third of a couple's property in the event of divorce. Prenups can override that benefit.

For reasons stated previously, it is important that the prenuptial agreement be coordinated with the couple's will. Using New York elective share as an example, if a man left all his property to his daughter in his will, his widow would have automatic right to one-third of that property unless the prenup stated otherwise. Usually when a couple marries, they draft a will or revise their existing wills and other documents. Ken Edelman notes that all documents, those pertaining to titling of assets, trusts, wills, life insurance, and so forth, need to be coordinated with the prenup.

Nothing in life is straightforward and as a couple's business and personal interests meld over the years, there are potentially vexing scenarios to consider when drafting the prenup. Although it's critical when entering into the contract to determine which properties are separate and which will be shared, what many people forget is that they have to keep the separate property separate after marriage. This becomes complicated, for example, when a summer home is designated the property of one party but the other party has contributed to its upkeep. At that point, assets have been commingled, making it more difficult to claim the residence as separate property.

Closely held businesses are another potential minefield. Edelman cautions that when designating ownership of such a business, couples need to be crystal-clear if one spouse is not to share in the future appreciation of the business. This was a critical issue for Jack King. He and his second wife had established a business and their prenup clearly defined her ownership percentage. Given the complexities of valuing small businesses, even with the prenup, couples need to have a valuation formula so the business won't have to be liquidated to meet the conditions of the prenup.

Some couples flirt with adding so-called lifestyle provisions in their prenups, but be aware that these can cause problems. Such provisions can range from who does the dishes to how many times per week a couple will enjoy marital relations. According to the experts, these issues are good to put on the table, but should not be included in the prenup. If the prenup is ever challenged, the courts will not enforce such private agreements, and they detract from the real reason for the prenuptial agreement, which is to protect each spouse financially. Prenups might be an ideal way for couples to initiate conversations about nonfinancial responsibilities and expectations, but they should remain separate from the legal contract. Edelman has even been asked by clients to include infidelity clauses that might state that the act of adultery is akin to initiating divorce. Again, he counsels against these, as they would be difficult to prove in court.

Dubin agrees and says she doesn't like these "bad boy or bad girl" clauses not only because they can be hard to prove, but also because "you never know who started what." If there is a provision in the prenup that the spouse who initiates the divorce gets a lesser amount, for example, it could be considered unfair because "sometimes the person who initiates divorce is actually the victim of abuse or infidelity," Dubin says.

Finally, prenuptial agreements don't have to live forever. Sunset provisions dictate that the agreement ends after a certain period of time. Sometimes couples will opt to enact their own sunset clause by breaking their prenuptial agreement, which can be done only if both parties agree in writing. This usually happens when a couple has been married a long time, says Edelman.

Charles Carson and his wife found the sunset provision to be the most difficult point to agree on when drafting their prenup. "She wanted ten years, and I wanted twenty," he says. In the end, they agreed on twenty years, but Carson is open to the possibility that they may want to break it earlier. According to Dubin, 60 percent of divorces occur in the first eight years of marriage, making sunset provisions a good source of comfort for some couples. "With the passage of time, there's a greater commitment," she says.

Conversely, if couples find that the original prenuptial agreement is outdated, they may want to redraft it, resulting in a postnuptial agreement. Postnuptial agreements (sometimes called internuptials or midnuptials) could be a smart strategy if a married couple wants to amend a prenuptial agreement or create an entirely new contract to clarify their financial and other contributions to the marriage. Common situations that might prompt a postnuptial agreement include the sale of a family business, receipt of an inheritance, or an agreement that one spouse will leave the workforce to care for children or elderly parents. They are usually not effective as a last-ditch effort to save a marriage, as seen in Ray Potter's case.

Although most states either have adopted or recognize some form of the UPAA, such is not the case with postnuptials. There is no act that applies specifically to them, though states may decide that the UPAA is valid for both, as in Colorado, where the laws regarding contractual agreements apply to postnuptials.

Ultimately, each couple needs to decide jointly if the terms of a prenuptial or postnuptial contract will stand the test of time. Although the documents, while successful, may prove incommodious, they are well worth it in the end, according to those who have successfully completed the negotiations. "The prenup doesn't stop after it's signed," says Charles Carson. "It takes on a positive air as it gives us the opportunity to continue to discuss finances and stay involved."

When the wealthy struggle with their own perception of money, as in Jane Newman's case, it is harder to flip the coin and look at the situation from the point of view of the less wealthy partner. If both partners have unhealthy associations with money, or can't come to a common philosophy about its place in their union, the problem will grow to outsize proportions and affect the next generation. When parents pass along mistrust or ignorance about money to their heirs, it prevents the children from using the wealth to develop their intellectual and human capital. If a new spouse coming into the family feels mistreated by the wealthier partner, those negative perceptions will likely preclude the family from having open and honest communication and will add a fissure to the family dynamics.

All of these issues will be resolved when a couple first agrees to a common philosophy about money and then works to equalize the estate to the extent that each partner feels at ease, using whichever method fits their needs. Then, communicating with the next generation and including them in the plan will help avoid nasty disagreements about the wealth.

As we will discover in Chapter 6, inheritors are at great risk for harboring guilt and ignorance around money, usually for the simple reason that they didn't earn it, and therefore lack the proper appreciation for their privileged state. When heirs enter into a relationship with unresolved feelings about wealth, they may react inappropriately to their partner's philosophy about money. It is incumbent on the first generation to overcome its own failings when it comes to wealth so they can teach their heirs sound money management and respect for the family's fortune.

PART III

Preparing Heirs

A s THE FOUNDER of the family fortune begins to plan for the transition of his hard-earned wealth, it is through the actions of the subsequent generations that his legacy will bear fruit. As mentioned in the Introduction, wealth in the hands of heirs can catapult families to greatness and the number of responsible heirs who are living out the founder's dreams and doing good is legion. The challenges for the founder are ensuring that his heirs don't feel a sense of *noblesse*, without the *oblige*, and that the wealth they inherit is not used to fund a wasteful and destructive life—the stuff that makes for so many made-for-TV movies.

Certainly America's "poor little rich girl," Barbara Hutton, did not set out to destroy the Woolworth department store fortune that her grandfather had built as a result of his hard work and ingenuity. Hutton's name wasn't always preceded by the *sobriquet* poor. At the time she inherited her fortune, on her 21st birthday, she was considered quite *lucky*. It was the early 1930s, and Hutton, an only child, immediately became one of the richest women in the world, subsequently a target for fortune hunters who took advantage of her low self-esteem.

Her mother's suicide, when Hutton was only 6 years old, left her in the custody of her successful businessman father, Franklin Laws Hutton, cofounder of the New York banking conglomerate E.F. Hutton & Company. Largely though, Barbara Hutton was raised by governesses and a succession of relatives. With no preparation for inheriting such a large fortune at a young age, Hutton became a victim of a life that led *her,* rather than the other way around. Married seven times and a serious drug addict, Hutton careened through life toward a tragic end, dying nearly destitute in 1979.

During her life, Hutton exhibited a propensity for generosity, giving both energy and money to supporting America's involvement in World War II. She gifted a London mansion and a yacht to the United States government and used her high-profile image to help sell war bonds. She casually gave gifts of her own fabulous jewelry to would-be admirers. Hutton's failings were her monumental lack of self-esteem and purpose. Without a fiscal education and no sense of responsibility toward her wealth, it was "easy come, easy go" for the inheritance. As a member of the third generation, she was a testament to the "rags to riches to rags in three generations" adage. Although she had a generous streak, and clearly favored worthy causes, she was not strategic in how she bestowed her fortune and consequently left no lasting public or family legacy.

In this section, the importance of fiscal education and psychological preparation surrounding an inheritance are told through the experiences of wealthy families. When parents don't set the stage for how to handle wealth, inheritors flounder. At best, heirs will maintain an arm's length distance from the money, afraid to touch it and not sure how to manage it. The family's hard-won fortune might even be a source of embarrassment as heirs strive to live on an equal footing with their peers and listlessly drift through career opportunities, all the while knowing that they don't really need to work. At worst, inheritors will view the money as a windfall to be spent quickly and solely for personal pleasure.

Preparation and education are also essential to the final two dilemmas in this section: parity among inheritors during estate planning and charitable bequests. As parents determine how to bequeath their fortune, they must at the same time consider how to treat their children justly or get the children to embrace their philanthropic initiatives if they plan to leave any part of the fortune to charity.

In Chapter 7 we'll examine the dilemma of "fair versus equal" when parents decide how to leave their legacy to children who display disparate levels of fiscal capability and responsibility. Given the inherent sibling rivalry in all families, parents walk a tightrope in divvying up assets when children apply zero-sum accounting to their inheritance: "if my sister gets more, it means I will get less."

The flip side, when the founder's vision for a legacy goes beyond the family, is our last dilemma. How does he persuade members of the clan to buy into his philanthropic initiatives if they know it means they will not get the money? According to Jay Hughes and other experts, there is a powerful dissenting urge among many in the family, especially from mom and the children, to keep the fortune for themselves and the founder is often unaware of this. As Hughes explains, when the founder seeks to leave his estate to charity, "this is an act of hubris because it perpetuates him forever" and others in the family may have trouble supporting his vision for immortality. "I have never known a wife to agree with her husband on this plan if she could find a way to head him off," Hughes adds. "Mothers do not like to benefit others ahead of their broods and generally find hubris an unenlightened male issue."

The challenge for the founder, then, is to recognize the possible negative reactions to his plan and ensure that everyone in the family understands and embraces his charitable interests if they are to be meaningful and sustaining. In this instance, it is wise for parents to teach children at a young age to appreciate philanthropy. A strategic approach to charitable intentions completes the education of both benefactor and children by allowing "hands-on" giving.

Part III of the family narrative is critical because it represents the point at which the generations who are far removed from the wealth creators are able to demonstrate the family's developmental success or failure and the force of the founder's vision and legacy. In families where common core values, communication, mission statements, governance, and mentoring have been strong and consistent, heirs will more than likely have a healthy and positive relationship with the wealth and ensure that it continues its generational journey.

Chapter Six

Preparing Children and Grandchildren

THE DILEMMA:

I need to prepare my children and grandchildren for the responsibility of wealth, but I'm afraid that if they know too much, it will destroy any initiative to earn a living. How do I communicate this concern?

ON THE ONE HAND, the fruits of the founder's labors have grown beyond his dreams. His hard work and modest lifestyle have garnered a fortune that can enrich the next generation and the one after that. On the other hand, the founder is about to bequeath the fortune to a generation that had no part in building the wealth and is only now on the cusp of earning its own way in life. Young adult heirs, the subject of this chapter, are ill equipped to assume the mantle of great wealth if they have not been educated about money. Furthermore, wealth generators are usually reluctant to hand over an amount of cash that is so large that is will prevent the inheritors from attaining the feelings of self-worth that they, the founders, enjoyed while amassing the family fortune.

The tension that this situation produces, little understood by those who don't have multigenerational wealth, is considerable for

153

the ultrarich. The final "rags" part of the "rags to riches to rags" adage can be devastating for families when they realize that they paved the way for their own undoing and let the wealth slip away through negligence. By failing to recognize that the perspective of the inheriting generation, so far removed from the source of the wealth, will be entirely different from that of the founder, the first two generations are shirking their responsibility to teach good stewardship to the heirs. What usually happens, whether from laziness or from a sense that money is a taboo topic, is that parents clam up and avoid doing anything, perhaps because they don't know how to approach the dilemma.

The danger in maintaining either of those stances is considerable for the next generation. According to the Social Welfare Research Institute, America is on the verge of the largest wealth transfer in history. Yet experts maintain that this wealth may be squandered, leaving well-intentioned wealth creators asking: How well have I prepared my heirs to take over this bounty? What obstacles am I creating for future generations of heirs who are striving to make their own way but are unable to find the motivation to work because the wealth is already theirs, packaged in neat trust funds?

Intermingled with the preparation of subsequent generations are issues of communication, financial education, and the powerhouses of self-esteem and productivity. Parents typically fear that if they tell the children they are rich, those same children will grow up believing they are better than their peers and that they do not have to work for a living. Experts maintain, however, that by not communicating about money and mentoring the next generation, the resulting confusion leads to either rampant spending without regard for the wealth or a timidity that causes the heirs to fear even acknowledging the money. In either case, wealth is not enhancing the lives of the beneficiaries nor is the money being used in a way that the founder might have envisioned.

In this chapter, we'll examine the dilemma of inheritance from the following angles, and from the viewpoints of the heirs, parents, and the experts (many of whom are inheritors themselves):

- *Making it on my own:* Don't underestimate the value of the self-esteem that results from earning a living.
- *Talking the talk:* Parents have to recognize the "elephant in the room" and not let conversations about money become taboo.
- *Walking the walk:* Parents set the best example for fiscal responsibility and offer guidance for assimilating wealth into their lives.

When the founders have clarified their intentions for the wealth and its use as a means to further the family's human and intellectual development, and they have designed a model for communicating and educating heirs, the transference of wealth has a more successful outcome for all generations. However, when founders take the view that "less is more" in terms of knowing about or talking about the wealth for fear that heirs will squander the money, they often unintentionally lead their offspring toward fulfilling that destiny.

Children usually have some sense that they are wealthy, even if the parents live modestly. But if their parents won't discuss the "elephant in the room," children probably won't ask questions and will miss out on learning even the simplest lessons about money. Eventually they will find themselves in a catch-up mode with regard to wealth management.

Grace Phillips (not her real name), who is 39, remembers the exact moment she learned she was an heiress. "I was on an airplane flight with my father when he pulled out a sheet of paper with all these financials." The document described a trust that her father had set up and he was explaining to her that she could choose to take the trust now, at age 21, or retain him as trustee until she was 28. "He just sort of laid it all out and I remember being in shock because I had no idea up to then."

Jerry Curtis, Phillips's father, expanded the family's wealth by building on the insurance business his father had founded and then selling it for millions of dollars. The family's lifestyle didn't reflect the windfall and Phillips and her sisters were raised in a relatively modest household. According to younger sister Pam Curtis, money was never really an issue nor was it ever discussed. "No one ever said, 'we can't afford that,' but we didn't live a luxurious life either."

Although the girls attended private schools, Curtis says the family had a station wagon and lived in a modest house. "The way I thought really rich people lived—we didn't live like that."

Wealth generators, like the sisters' grandfather and father, who struggled to build an empire from the ground up, either want their children to grow up with the same paucity of materialism that they experienced or they try to compensate for their own impoverished background by meeting their child's every demand. In both scenarios, potential heirs experience a lack of motivation to make their own living and to learn the skills necessary for managing wealth.

Making It on My Own

When it comes to money, does not earning a living preclude a sense of worth? Talk to inheritors and the answer seems to be yes. Haunted by terms like idle rich and trust-fund babies, inheritors grapple with the psychological ramifications of a fortune they received without ever having to lift a finger and in many cases, without knowing how to fit the wealth into their lives.

Jessie O'Neill, MA, a wealth counselor and author of *The Golden Ghetto,* taps into her own experiences as an heiress to counsel others. She says inheritors often have a sense of guilt and shame that comes from the knowledge that they didn't make the money that supports them. This leads to the sense that "I didn't earn it, so I probably don't deserve it." What most people don't understand, even the very wealthy, O'Neill says, is that the freedom that comes with money can also be terrifying. "If you're young and unprepared, there are so many choices, you're overwhelmed, or you use it for the wrong things—fast money, fast cars, fast women."

O'Neill's family's money came from her grandfather's tenure as president of General Motors. Her experience overcoming her own addictive behaviors led her to counsel wealthy dysfunctional families dealing with some of the same behaviors—excessive buying and spending. O'Neill is a potent example of what a sudden influx of money can do to a young person with low self-esteem and substance abuse problems. The money becomes an enabler. The ease with which inheritors can buy the means to continue a personal descent makes it harder for them to surface and see the light, as O'Neill eventually did.

Armed with an inheritance at age 18, O'Neill worked only part-time. The untimely death of her mother, at age 54 when O'Neill was 28, provided her with yet another bundle of money—enough to live on without having to work. Stuck in a quagmire of low self-esteem, the money simply enabled her to continue her self-destructive life-style and dysfunctional behavior. As a result, she recommends that heirs should not receive their inheritances until they are at least in their 30s so they can spend their 20s developing a solid work ethic and respect for money. Giving money earlier only provides a dis-traction from gainful employment. "It's hard to get motivated with money. If they don't have to get out of bed, they won't," she says. On the other hand, it doesn't have to be a paid job that provides motivation. O'Neill points out that it's only necessary for inheritors to find the motivation in their heart—there are heirs who do work that contributes to the general welfare of society, but who don't get paid for it.

The other scenario when heirs are given too much too soon is less horrifying, but still not good. A paralyzing hesitancy grows out of feelings of inadequacy when it comes to managing money and the knowledge that they don't have to work for a living. As adults, the heirs feel inadequate and worthless compared to their peers who have forged a career. Once again, lack of preparation and communi-cation about wealth are at the root of the problem.

Barbara Blouin, author and founder of The Inheritance Project, which explores issues concerning inherited wealth, is herself a first-generation heir. Over the years, she has overcome her negative feel-ings about money, eventually gaining control of an irrevocable trust and learning to manage her wealth. Blouin and O'Neill have similar stories in that neither had received enough positive attention grow-ing up to foster self-esteem. Blouin's parents also never spoke to her about money. Probably from a sense of parental duty, and with one eye toward saving estate taxes, they set up an irrevocable trust that gave her an income but didn't allow her any input or understanding into what was happening with her money.

Feeding off the income from her trust fund, she tried not to let her friends know she was wealthy. For Blouin, "keeping up with the Joneses" meant living below her means as a way of fitting in with her friends. She wishes now that she had been forced to work. "If I had had to work, I would have developed a career or something I could do, and that part of my life would have been fulfilling, but it wasn't," she says. "I would have gotten it together but I didn't because I didn't have to."

Coupled with the lack of communication is a suspicion that the founding generation doesn't trust the next one to be able to handle financial matters intelligently. Especially when given an income from a trust created by parents, inheritors are denied the opportunity to prove their worth by forging ahead with that particularly American ethos of creating an identity and being able to declare "I made it." Blouin says, "Our society is based on being good at work and making money, and when you're not doing that, it's awkward and painful. It's especially difficult for people in their 20s who are still finding their identities."

Pam Curtis concurs and says, "I feel really uncomfortable with the question, 'what do you do?' I say I've been taking classes or I'll tell them where I've been recently. Some people think it's great that I have that freedom and others keep pushing to know, and so I'll say I have some money from family investments." Like Blouin, Curtis maintains a low-key lifestyle, more in line with that of her friends. She is still taking classes, trying to figure out what to do. "I'd like to work for myself on my own schedule and work one-on-one with other people." Meanwhile, income from the trust allows her to live comfortably. "It turned out I didn't have to work, but that's not really been fulfilling for me," she says. She recalls that when her father told her about her money, they were rafting down the Colorado River. "He didn't call it a trust fund, he said 'when you turn 21, you'll receive some investments that Granddad and I set up for you and your sisters, and you'll have some income.'" Her father also informed her that her older sister, Grace Phillips, had decided to keep him as trustee and Curtis followed suit. When she was 28, she had to make the choice again and chose to let her father remain as trustee for another seven years. It's only been lately, with her father still acting as trustee, that she's becoming more involved in learning about her financial situation.

Curtis and Phillips are close to their parents and both women report that their father is doing an excellent job safeguarding their money and explaining the balance sheets. Curtis speculates that her father's protective stance toward his daughters stems from his own experience as a business tycoon. When he was telling her about the investments, the intention was that she should use the money to discover what she really enjoyed doing, but that she would also have a job. As it turned out, the investment portfolio did well and she's able to live off it. Her father told her that his philosophy is that travel, education, giving back to society, and life experiences are important. "When he was growing up, he had the pressure to follow in his father's footsteps," Curtis says. "He didn't want his three daughters to be workaholics, but he wanted us to find work that was meaningful to us."

By encouraging his daughters to pursue their own interests, their father was giving them what he considered a great gift. Jerry Curtis was not an inheritor; he worked hard to make the business a success. When he was at the point in his life where he could present a gift of money to his children, he viewed it as just that—a gift. Lack of enthusiasm on the part of Phillips or Curtis would have made them ingrates in his mind. Yet, the next generation ends up struggling with confusion, surprise, and an inability to manage the "gift" responsibly. This situation is foreign to the founder because his experience was so vastly different.

Often, young people need to focus their drive on a single career path or they end up drifting along through whatever seems interesting at the time and they never work toward a sustainable goal. By not being required to earn a living, even at a career they may only be "trying on," the heirs fail to gain the sense of control over their lives that comes with knowing they will always be able to support themselves.

Although Curtis knows she's fortunate to be able to pursue her interests, the drawbacks of receiving inherited income so early, she says, are that "a lot of times I feel scattered. I am very responsible by nature, yet I've been able to live a life devoid of responsibility. A lot has to do with living in more than one place and traveling. If I didn't have as many choices as I do, I may have developed more skills." This is a shared sentiment, say many inheritors.

The money provides the possibility of exploration, but often the age of majority, at 18 or 21, is a time when structure is needed. Forced to stick to a plan that will lead to a goal gives young adults a sense of control and accomplishment. The receipt of a trust income can help inheritors reject situations that don't appeal to them, which can have both positive and negative consequences. The possibility of wealth means that heirs can pursue the careers they're passionate about without worrying about the salary. But for those who are adrift, the drive to succeed can itself be a lifeline.

Curtis says that having money is, for her, "like a big safety net. It allows you to avoid uncomfortable situations, which can inhibit your emotional growth because you can pay to change it. If I'm bored or I just don't like the weather, I can pick up and move." She talks about a van she once owned. "I probably put about 50,000 miles on it, but if it broke down, I could just buy another one. I don't have to wait around for a week to have it fixed."

Another problem plaguing inheritors who receive money early is that they may never learn to manage it. When someone else has made the money, then packaged it in a format that allows him or her to retain control (as with many trusts), inheritors might never view it as theirs. This can lead to wasted opportunities for using the wealth to advance the next generation's human, intellectual, and financial capital.

Grace Phillips says there is less pressure for her to work because she is raising her own children. She has other reasons for not being more proactive in managing her trust fund. Labeling herself a "financial avoider," she concludes, "I just didn't want to have to deal with it and be responsible for it. I need to take more control, and I'm learning about finances, but I'm indecisive by personality."

Despite her pecuniary reluctance, she says, "it's important for me as a female to be financially savvy. I know what's in my portfolio, and I just let it sit. I'm not a big risk-taker." Because she doesn't have a salary, she finds the income from her trust liberating. "I feel so blessed and it's so freeing to not have to ask my husband for an allowance." She pays for groceries, clothes for her and the kids, and some other things. Her husband, an attorney, pays for the medical and house insurance, and various other expenses. "I'm not confined within his salary," she says. "If he wants to buy a new bicycle for the triathlons he competes in, he uses his own money. It's great for both of us."

Phillips is learning the benefits of wealth, but she understands the need to go a step further by taking a hard look at her family situation and trying to teach her own children to understand and appreciate wealth. As an inheritor responsible for the family's only fourth-generation members, Phillips is warily guiding her children into uncharted waters, while trying to learn from the mistakes of the first generation, whose errors in judgment she sees played out in the family meetings. "At the last family meeting, my father says these nice things about what we've done, but no one has really accomplished anything," she says. Phillips is doing some creative writing, but she wants her children to learn the value of work earlier than she did. She recognizes the pitfalls of subsequent generations not appreciating the power of money to facilitate a family's downfall.

"Our family is the classic example of what you hear about," she laments. "My grandfather started the company in the early 1930s and then my father worked there and built the business. He sold it to a larger corporation and now the wealth is in the third generation. But for most of my cousins, it has not been beneficial." Some of the cousins spent without any purpose and are now poor. Other cousins, enabled by money that precluded their having to work, made bad choices. "I want to break that tradition with my own children. With them, I will probably go more toward the way my husband's family raised him," she adds. "I want them to know the value of a job and how rewarding it is."

Phillips and her sister Pam Curtis agree that the mistake their own parents made was "in not having expectations for us." Their clothes may have come from Sears, like all the other kids at school, but they weren't expected to have summer jobs. Phillips's and Curtis's parents set an admirable example of not letting the wealth overtake them, and they instilled in their children the value of living a life in which money is not the "end-all-be-all" that many think will transform them into better people with richer lives. However, with some communication and fiscal preparation, Phillips and Curtis might not be struggling still to incorporate the wealth into their lives. As Curtis said earlier, there was precious little discussion of money while they were growing up. The family meetings would have been an ideal setting for a financial curriculum.

Talking the Talk

Parents have to break the great taboo and have conversations about money. Signs of impending fiscal irresponsibility loom large for parents who haven't figured out how to broach the subject of the family fortune. Afraid of the nightmarish bragging rights that come with elevated circumstances—"it's not just about the money, it's *all* about the money"—parents worry that their children will live out the modern-day version of Jay Gatsby's life of leisure and excess.

Take the film *Born Rich*, directed by Jamie Johnson, scion of the Johnson & Johnson pharmaceutical giant. The documentary generated buzz in wealthy circles for exposing a subject more taboo than sex—namely, wealth. Johnson broke with tradition to stare down the family secret and publicly ask the question "Why doesn't our family talk about money? If we don't talk about it," he remarks wistfully to his father, "how will we ever know how we feel about it?"

In the film, Johnson's contemporaries render their feelings about money in spades, much to the chagrin of the old guard. Confusion, panic, and rampant acquisitiveness taint the attitudes of the interviewees, many of whom who are barely of legal age. Few of the inheritors in the film appear prepared to handle the family's masses of wealth. For his part, Johnson laments, "The thing is, nobody wants to talk about money." That's why he wants to talk to his peers about "the subject everybody knows is not polite to talk about." In the film, Johnson reveals that he learned his family was wealthy when he was

10 years old. A fourth-grade classmate found his father's name in *Forbes* magazine's list of the 400 richest people. "I felt like I was being told a secret that I wasn't supposed to know."

Avoiding any discussion about the "family secret" is common among the very group that should be preparing their heirs. This laissez-faire attitude is the spur that drives Jessie O'Neill and Barbara Blouin to help others sidestep their own experiences and become psychologically equipped to handle being born rich. "I wasn't given any preparation to be an heir," recalls Blouin. "Many children are not prepared well, or at all, because parents don't want to talk about money." Consequently, when the heirs receive a trust fund, "it blows them away." O'Neill concurs, "It's the norm not to talk about money."

Timing a discussion about money depends on the children's maturity, but the earlier the better. "It's kind of like sex. If their eyes glaze over, you've said too much," O'Neill says. But at every age, children can express feelings about their wealth. "How does a third-grader feel about living in a big house when her best friend lives in an apartment? If they can't say it, they can draw a picture." Once parents know the child's feelings, they can broaden the definition of wealth by talking about such attributes as kindness, humor, good health, and a fulfilling family life. Again, family meetings can provide a consistent dedicated time for parents to instruct and listen.

In an open environment, like a family meeting, where heirs are encouraged to talk about money, parents must be prepared to answer all types of questions, and fend off those they think might be too specific, such as telling young children just how much money the family actually has. If children aren't allowed to ask any questions, however, parents won't know what they are thinking and will be unable to deal with potential problems down the road. O'Neill favors disclosing the amount of inheritance in discussions when children are old enough to understand. "Being an heir myself, I could have had financial people in place and been prepared. Had I known, I would have made wiser choices."

Preemptive communication affords another benefit, according to O'Neill. "It adds to the education of the kids so they have insight into the hopes, dreams, and values" of the family founders. "There is a whole school of thought that says you'll ruin kids if you tell them about money," says Joline Godfrey, author of *Raising Financially Fit Kids*, and CEO of Independent Means Inc. "Those children know they're trust-fund kids, whether you tell them or not." Godfrey says that if parents don't talk to their children about money, "they set up a 'waiting for the lottery' mindset that puts kids in a waiting mode to buy and in the meantime, they're not acquiring any skills about managing money."

Being unsophisticated about money in this day and age is dangerous, Godfrey counsels. Parents who don't want to talk to their kids about money have no excuses. "I tell reluctant parents that your children are living in a world where everyone is talking about money and they may pick up messages from others that you don't agree with. They're also growing up in a global village, and your children may be left behind because of competition from the rest of the world. The Chinese, for example, put enormous resources into teaching their kids entrepreneurship."

Parents who want to control the messages their children receive about money need to start talking early, realizing that by doing so, they are staving off future irresponsibility and confusion. As we see later, it's not always easy to just talk, but it's a start. Parents can always seek outside counsel for ways to begin the discussion.

Walking the Walk

Parents set the best example for fiscal responsibility and offer guidance on assimilating wealth into their lives. In addition to deconstructing the myth of wealth through communication, families need to demonstrate their resolve to allow, or in some cases, force their children to be productive. The journey may prove to be arduous because parents have to put aside any lingering reluctance to communicate and make the effort to instruct their offspring consistently. The results are enormously gratifying when the heirs develop into self-supporting individuals with a healthy attitude toward wealth.

As a result of her parents' diligence in dealing with the so-called elephant in the room, Claire Johnson (not her real name), a 22-year-old student from Florida, views a potential inheritance from her parents as "icing on the cake." As she says, "If I receive an inheritance, I don't think I'll live off it. My parents are young and healthy, and by the time I get it, I don't think I'll need it. But I'd like to build on it for my children." She and her twin brother "were forced to act like kids who weren't going to inherit money."

When the children were older, John and Carrie Johnson established a foundation and got the kids involved from the start. The twins tagged along to meetings with organizations that had requested funding and were encouraged to develop ideas for charities they wanted to support with resources of both time and money. The twins were instrumental in developing the foundation's mission statement and its website. During their teen years, the siblings sometimes complained about attending family meetings and investigating various charities that were seeking the foundation's support, but Carrie Johnson held fast to her belief that involvement was a good way to instill in them wealth's larger benefits.

With the help of family wealth advisers, the couple spent time teaching their children fiscal responsibility. They required weekly written budgets while the twins were in college. The Johnson offspring learned about their modest trust funds and had investment policy meetings with the family's wealth advisers, beginning when they were in their teens. The Johnsons have told the twins that most of the family wealth will funnel to the foundation. Now college graduates, the twins are expected to make their own way. Claire Johnson is headed for graduate school and a business degree, while her brother is taking time to work in an orphanage. Because of the Johnsons' dedication in not only talking about wealth, but also in imparting their beliefs about the good the money can do, they have avoided the pitfalls of confusion and strife over the money and have provided role models of behavior for the second generation to draw on when they counsel their own children.

Sometimes, the impetus for fiscal education comes from the heir, making it easier for the parent to respond to a child's ready-made curiosity. Greg Burgon (not his real name), a college student in New

York City, became interested in the family's business and in investing when he was around 12 years old. Working with the family's wealth adviser, he began learning about stock markets. "We visited the New York Stock Exchange," he says. "It was Investing 101."

As a child, Burgon had been curious about finance and his mother responded to his interest by finding ways to help him learn more. Burgon learned that with his interest came the expectation of increased responsibility. Details about the family's diverse holdings weren't immediately available to him. "The feeling in my family is that people don't get to know the numbers until the family elders (his mother and her two sisters) think we can handle it. I was in tenth grade before I saw a complete balance sheet," he says. "After I turned 18, I was invited to attend shareholder meetings. I've been going to them for the last three years. I almost feel like it's a responsibility to learn."

The result of the mentoring Burgon received is that he exhibits a healthy attitude toward his inheritance. "I feel like the wealth provides some freedom to pursue a career not just for monetary purposes," he says. "I want to go to graduate school and get a PhD in nanotechnology. Ideally, I'd like to do research for a company or at a university or manage an engineering firm."

When the younger generations show signs of behaving like supplicants at the feet of Socrates, financial preparation glides into place. Yet, as any parent knows, birds of a feather don't always flock together. Greg Burgon's younger brother, Joe, is a totally different kind of bird. Following more usual adolescent pursuits, Joe Burgon is interested in what he can buy immediately rather than what he can save.

"We're starting to work with him," says their mother, Gina Burgon. "As a seventh-grader, Greg would pay attention at meetings and have critical thoughts afterward," she says. Joe Burgon is more the typical teen. "All he cares about is knowing how much money he's going to be able to spend."

By talking to her children, and observing their behavior when it comes to money, Gina Burgon knows that her second son will require a different education. Although she didn't have to teach fiscal restraint to her older son, she has been diligent with the younger one and is seeing signs of frugality since she put him on an allowance that forces him to budget for some of the things he wants. "When he goes to the movies with his friends, he won't blow his money on the big popcorn and soda," she says. "He's learning to hold some money back for something he might want tomorrow."

Among Gina Burgon's worries is a problem many founders encounter—unanticipated trust-fund payouts. Certain trusts, popular with business owners, can end up distributing much more than was intended if the original investment does well. Sometimes the trusts were established by grandparents or parents who didn't give much thought to when the heirs would be able to lay claim to the money and the resulting distribution looks like a fortune to a teen who cares only about the latest Prada handbag or Lamborghini sports car.

Funds from such a trust will pay out to Joe Burgon as early as next year. A company the family had invested in has done well and Gina Burgon has been making annual gifts to trusts for minors in the names of both boys. She estimates the trusts will pay tens of thousands of dollars annually. "That can look like a lot of money to a 17- or 18-year-old," she says. The trust distribution is something Gina Burgon, her husband, and her son need to put on the table for discussion, she adds. Family meetings are an excellent venue for these discussions.

"My second son is a typical teenager, currently into minimizing effort," says Gina Burgon. She wants him to create another trust fund, as her older son did a few years ago, with the understanding that it can grow and eventually finance the purchase of something of greater value, like a home. "But we don't want him to think we're taking the money away from him." Family meetings can help here as well. In a relaxed environment, with everyone primed to listen, heirs can talk about their intentions for the money, and parents can respond with creative ways to help them meet their goals while still remaining fiscally responsible and saving for the future. For example, when a 16-year-old with a payout from a trust fund salivates over a sports car, parents can set limits and preempt any rash behavior with a fiscal education curriculum. When children learn about budgeting, investing, and philanthropy as well as goal setting and delayed gratification, they might begin to see the light when it comes to managing money. The trick is to be consistent, obtain outside help if needed, and be a good role model.

The difference between a prepared inheritor and a financial disaster waiting to happen is rooted in communication and trust on the part of the first generation. Building trust takes time and patience and is best accomplished in baby steps. Gina Burgon thinks giving children an allowance, as she has done, enables them to make their own small mistakes early and provides crucial control over money. She has already noticed her second son becoming more aware of his spending habits when it's his own money. Burgon adds that when she was younger, "we (she and her siblings) never really had much control. My parents would pay for the things we needed and wanted. We probably got more that way. I learned with my kids that if they have control, they spend less. If I pay for it, I spend more." Granting youngsters control over some money, she adds, also helps them learn that not every whim needs to be satisfied. "I wish I had known that sometimes short-term fixes are not worth it in the long term." A wealthy family faced with the choice between a child's summer job or a family trip to Europe, for example, would probably take the easy way out. "I know I do that all the time as a parent because I want to take the family vacation." Instead, those who sacrifice the vacation for a job are making a choice that is more in line with the family's long-term objectives.

Joline Godfrey agrees that an allowance is "an important tool for helping kids learn to manage money. It's not an entitlement or a salary but a way to practice money management skills. It's not for kids to spend any way they like but a way to prove to the parents that they have learned the skills." Godfrey says it's never too early to teach children about money. She recommends beginning when they are 5 years old, and calls the years between 5 and 18 an "apprenticeship." The education process is iterative, she says, and likens it to teaching a foreign language. "You wouldn't expect a child to know Spanish in a week or a month."

Even if parents have neglected to start their children on the road to financial wisdom early, it's never too late. "Don't despair," says Godfrey. "This process is developmental, not chronological. You still start at the beginning, but it will go faster. Once you get kids started, they will learn a lot of this on their own." For teens, who are often loath to sit and listen to a lecture, Godfrey has found an alternative method in sending them on retreats or into the family business to get hands-on experience. This was the method favored by Greg Burgon, who visited the New York Stock Exchange and has also been learning while participating in the family business.

"As a general rule, an intense experience tends to be the best intervention," says Godfrey. "Nothing succeeds like having an experience. It's one thing to listen to Mom and Dad, and another to do it yourself." Godfrey lists the ten basic money skills that should be taught to children, beginning at the age when they can understand and handle each one.

1) How to save.
2) How to keep track of money.
3) How to get paid what you are worth.
4) How to spend wisely.
5) How to talk about money.
6) How to live within a budget.
7) How to invest.
8) How to exercise the entrepreneurial spirit.
9) How to handle credit.
10) How to use money to change the world.

She says that the different developmental stages of children dictate which tasks they can master. For example, in the earliest stage, between 5 and 8 years old, children are curious but have short attention spans. They can learn to count money and to differentiate between "want" and "need." By stage four, the late teen years, they have an increased capacity for logic and are experimenting with independence. They can learn to save, spend and invest, connect goals with money, and exhibit a developing capacity for economic self-sufficiency by writing checks or completing simple tax forms.

When parents follow a dedicated financial road map for their children, such as the one Godfrey offers, their ability to handle an inheritance, and to give it proper perspective in their lives, will be greatly enhanced.

Once again, founders have to practice caution when setting up trusts or accounts for children or grandchildren. Certain vehicles that look good for tax reasons or as a place to park low-basis company stock can balloon to proportions far beyond expectations by the time a child is legally able to take a distribution. If children have had no fiscal education, trying to convince them to roll the money into a new trust or postponing withdrawal will be futile. Furthermore, all the experts agree that giving millions of dollars to heirs too early—even well prepared heirs—is a classic mistake. Let the next generation earn money during their 20s, while they can appreciate the value of work, and earn self-esteem.

Sometimes, parents in the second generation are surprised by the founder's treatment of the third generation. Barbara Blouin says that her son received a sum from a Uniform Gift to Minor's Act trust fund that her father had established. But Blouin wasn't aware of it until her son was nearly 18. "I was mad as hell at my father for doing that," she says. The trust, a vehicle for saving on estate taxes for the first generation, "infantilizes" the second, because the inherent message is that they cannot be trusted to manage the money for their own children. More important, perhaps, was that Blouin had no time to prepare her son for the windfall. Blouin counsels parents to be diligent, and to think about their actions and the unspoken messages they send. Action, she says, really does speak louder than words when it comes to fiscal education. "Don't spoil children, practice what you preach, have expectations, set boundaries, and give lots of love," she says. She favors working with wealth counselors when deciding when and how to tell children about an inheritance. Give the subsequent generations conditions for the inheritance, she says, and only after they've had time to "earn and learn."

Even though irrevocable trusts that begin payouts at the age of maturity are good estate-planning vehicles for parents, Blouin frowns on them because they don't allow the children any control.

"They feel like they're always under someone's thumb," she says. Far better are the so-called stepped-in trusts, she thinks, which distribute small amounts at various ages. Blouin doesn't rule out handing over money directly, which can be a risky but effective tutorial. She gave her younger son money when he was 24 because he had seen his older stepbrother being favored with a monetary gift from their grandfather. Blouin had no control over the actions of her father, but she could try to level the playing field herself by giving the younger son the gift. "There were no strings attached," she says. "I don't know what he did with it. I suspect he spent it quickly. But if the parent is prepared to have a certain amount of money vanish, it can be a very good learning experience." Once the money is spent, it's gone.

Finally, Blouin counsels that at a very young age children can be taught a classic rule that John D. Rockefeller ingrained in his family—put a percentage of their allowance into the bank, give some to a charity of their choice, and spend a portion. Rockefeller advised allocating one-third to each. Balance, wise investment, and a wider view of the role of money are the lessons to be learned by this system.

For all the education provided by counselors, and the common sense gleaned by parents who have gone through their own struggles with wealth, inheritors pass along some insight from what they observe among their peers and the lessons learned from their parents. Note that the advice they give from their own experience is the same as that offered by the experts.

Educate children about budgeting and saving, says Claire Johnson. "I've seen kids who spend hundreds of dollars a week on cocaine. How do parents not ask them about where the money is going? Where do they think (the money) is being spent? It's irresponsible of parents, "she adds, "you can't just give kids a credit card and say 'go.'"

Children should earn their own living. They shouldn't have so much money that they never learn how to support themselves. Neither Greg Burgon nor Claire Johnson thinks their inheritance will give them enough to rely on without additional employment.

Make individual decisions about how much to tell children

based on their maturity. Burgon and Johnson are not opposed to trust funds if they can establish them for themselves. Burgon says he has two trust funds; his grandmother set up one and he established the other, when he was 18, with the proceeds from a trust for minors from his mother. He can tap into it if he needs to, but it is not meant for day-to-day expenses. "If I were to decide to take a year to study art in Italy, I could talk to the trustee." Potential heirs should know about the family wealth, urges Burgon. "It's a disservice to them not to tell them because they're going to have to deal with it eventually."

As a final determination of heir readiness, Roy Williams and Vic Preisser have developed checklists that prove to be valuable aids. They were designed for parents and potential heirs to use. Once

---

HEIR READINESS CHECKLIST FOR PARENT/OWNERS

1. Has a FAMILY WEALTH MISSION been developed with the involvement of the entire family and spouses?

2. Has a STRATEGY to implement the Family Wealth Mission Statement been decided on?

3. Have the ROLES needed to carry out that strategy been defined?

4. Are there specific observable and measurable STANDARDS in place to determine qualifications for each role?
   - Education
   - Experience
   - Family Relationship

5. Has the COMPETENCE LEVEL required for each role been clearly defined (in the range of "Beginner" to "Virtuoso")?

6. Are the heirs and the current family leaders in AGREEMENT on the application of "Standards" and "Competencies" for the defined roles as essential to the success of the Family Wealth Mission?

7. Have heirs selected specific roles and DECLARED THEIR INTEREST in preparing for and serving in those roles?

completed, the lists can be a jumping-off place for discussion by the family council or during informal family meetings, as families determine what steps need to be taken for the successful transfer of wealth.

"These are individual assessments—for either Mom and Dad or for the kids," says Roy Williams. They provide a comparison of how a family stacks up against the 3,250 other wealthy families that Williams studied to determine what is needed for a successful wealth transfer. Williams's findings are worth repeating here. For 70 percent of the families studied, wealth did not transfer successfully to the next generation. Within that group, 60 percent lost both their wealth and their family harmony due to a breakdown in communication and trust within the family; 25 percent had failed to adequately

---

8. Have conflicts between heirs who may be ASPIRING TO THE SAME ROLE been amicably resolved?

---

9. Has a specific PROGRAM OF PREPARATION been designed and accepted by heirs designated as candidates for identified roles?

---

10. Is the program of preparation under way, with agreed-on ALTERNATIVES for each candidate-heir, in the event his/her Preparation timetable or completeness for a role is unmet?

Scoring: The Heir Readiness Checklist is approximately sequential. All ten questions should ultimately be answered "YES." Those estates in which heirs with the ability to answer all ten questions "yes" will have minimized the risk of failure in transitioning their wealth. It is not simply the "knowing" that is critical, it is the conversion of knowledge into action ("doing") that offsets the risk that heirs will be damaged, or might lead the family estate to ultimate failure. For that reason, the above checklist carries with it a presumption that the family works on (and maintains) a high level of trust and communication within the family, keeps updating and referencing the family wealth mission, and closely follows the preparation course of action being followed by the heir(s). Only with that close attention to preparing heirs for wealth with responsibility can the family move its estate from the "likely to fail" group into the "likely to succeed" group.

READINESS SELF-CHECKLIST FOR HEIRS

1. Have I worked with my parent(s) and other family members to define a clear long-term MISSION for the family wealth?

2. Have I actively worked with my family to develop the STRATEGY for achieving the mission of the family wealth?

3. Have the various ROLES for the management of the family assets been identified, and do I support filling those ROLES with fully competent individuals?

4. Do I know what my PERSONAL INTERESTS are, and understand my ABILITIES well enough to identify a specific role for myself?

5. In preparing for a particular role, am I willing to be evaluated against specific observable and measurable STANDARDS?
   • Education (formal and informal)
   • Experience (task, competitive, charitable)
   • Family Relationships (building, strengthening)

6. Have I selected a MENTOR whom I respect, who cares about my personal fulfillment, but who will be honest with me with respect to my contributions to the family mission?

7. Have I developed, with my Mentor, a specific plan to become COMPETENT for the family mission role that satisfies my interests and talents, within the mission staffing timeframe?

---

prepare the heirs; and "all other causes," including tax and legal issues, account for the remaining 15 percent.

In the end, it's the many facets of communication and education that will enable inheritors to enjoy wealth in a productive manner. Founders and second-generation parents must participate in setting the ground rules for the multigenerational narrative. If they have anticipated the future generations' attitudes and potential pitfalls, they can begin to design a structure that will safeguard the wealth. Blithely handing it over in the form of a trust that pays out a large amount at an early age is usually not the best answer.

The family council can assist with scheduling, income amounts, education, and qualifications for inheritors. When inheritors under-

8. Am I EMOTIONALLY OPEN to the communications requirements and the continuing learning and evaluation that is required of each role-occupying individual within the family wealth mission structure?

9. Do I clearly understand the difference between KNOWING (what needs to be done) versus DOING (what needs to be done) and to discipline myself to act in the best interests of the mission?

10. Have I assumed personal responsibility for learning from the unavoidable "BUMPS IN THE ROAD" as demonstrated by developing (and maintaining) the skills to strengthen my family during difficult times?

Scoring: The steps above are basic to gauging an heir's personal progress in preparing for the responsibility of wealth. Fully prepared heirs will have "YES" answers to all checklist items, and the heir's mentor will be in agreement with those scores. This greatly reduces the risk of failure in preparing for and assuming responsibilities for family wealth and values. The worldwide data is incontrovertible—70 percent of wealth transitions will fail. The careful preparation of heirs, accompanied by learned skills and practiced behavior of communications and trust within the family are critical to the 30 percent that succeed.

These generalized preparation questions are valid whether the heir has a role in financial management, financial management oversight, or is actively working in the family enterprise itself, including the family foundation. The above steps are listed in somewhat sequential form and can be used as a year-to-year measurement of progress.

From: *Preparing Heirs*, © 2003, Williams & Preisser, p. 138. Used by permission.

stand that there is a process and responsibility for managing wealth, reinforced through the example of their elders, they will be more likely to want to take part in continuing the legacy and enhancing all forms of their family's capital.

In the next chapter, we look at another dilemma related to leaving an inheritance—how to do it in a way that makes the heirs feel they are being treated fairly. No matter what the founder's plans are for the money, whether the assets are divided equally or more is planned for a child with a perceived greater need, each heir needs to understand the intentions of the founder in order to lessen the ugly consequences of sibling rivalry.

Chapter 7 Seven

Fairness in Estate Planning

THE DILEMMA:

I plan to be fair to my children, but if I leave them unequal amounts of money, am I setting up a future battleground?

FAIR ISN'T ALWAYS equal in estate planning. The quandary for parents is how to treat the next generation equitably, even if the monetary amount that each child receives is unequal. Maintaining family harmony in such situations is tricky because heirs so often equate the money their parents leave after they die with the love they feel they received when their parents were alive.

Sibling rivalry is ingrained in human culture. A close look at nature reveals that humans aren't the only creatures who compete with their brothers and sisters. Some species of infant birds, for example, will actually peck a weaker sibling to death or push it out of the nest. Darwin's theory of survival of the fittest is carried to the nth degree where there are no discernable moral values. In human families children obviously aren't justified in killing each other, no matter how quickly competition escalates. But with such a powerful instinct for rivalry, the pecking takes the form of seemingly endless litigation when the monetary stakes are high. Siblings may also try to push the other "out of the nest" by severing relationships and splitting the family for subsequent generations who might never get to know the banished uncle or aunt.

In wealthy families, where there is a substantial amount of money to pass on, children quickly learn to equate what their parents give them with the love they think they are entitled to, and the bequests become the tangible manifestation of that parental love. Just watch young children on Christmas morning mentally check off the number of presents each one has received to make sure they received as much or more than the next one. The dilemma for wealthy families who decide to bequeath their fortune to their children is to find a way to do it so that each child is provided for, and that fiscal responsibility and trustworthiness are rewarded. It also means structuring the bequests to those without good judgment or financial skills in a way that gives them an opportunity to improve. In seeking ways to solve this dilemma, we will examine the following issues:

- *Seeking equality:* Fair is not always equal in estate planning; yet children will sometimes associate inheritance with love.
- *Clarifying your intentions:* When parents talk about their philosophy around money, they leave no doubts as to their intentions.
- *Structuring the bequests:* Parents can choose among a variety of methods to show their intentions for the inheritance.

The issue of fairness among children has plagued us for generations and as long as there are families, there will be distributions that are perhaps unequal yet equitable, attorney Lisa Schneider points out. "All children are not created equal. They may be born to the same parents and given the same opportunities, but they are each dealt a different hand in life. Some parents determine that life differences do not warrant an unequal division of assets, whereas some try to balance these inequalities the last time they can, at death."

Competition for parental attention doesn't make it any easier for the older generation to make the tough estate-planning decisions. "Throughout life, parents are accused of 'favoring the baby,' 'demanding more of the eldest,' and 'not having enough time for the middle child,'" says Schneider. "Each child is different from the others, regardless of what they have been given. But will this individualized treatment cause resentment even when the well-to-do child does not need the money as much as her special-needs sibling? And what if one child has chosen to remain childless and the other has so many that life is an economic roller-coaster?"

Seeking Equality

Even those children who are involved in the estate-planning process can "forget" what they agreed to after the parents are gone, signifying the importance seemingly nonchalant children place on being treated equally. Alison Lake (not her real name) tells the story of her own family's problems resulting from the surprising reaction of her mother, Tina Smith, to the estate plan of Smith's parents.

Tim Smith, Lake's father, and his family had built a business that made the family wealthy. When Tim and Tina married, "the company was doing great and on the verge of a major expansion. They had caught a big wave, and everyone knew it." Tim Smith suggested to his wife that they tell her parents to leave their estate to their two sons because Tina would be taken care of by Tim and the Smith family wealth. "My mother agreed to the suggestion," Lake continues. "My grandfather on my mother's side was a good worker, but with a mid-level job. When my grandfather died, he left his modest estate to his two sons, as planned. One son was an attorney and had, in fact, written the will. My mother was furious, even to this day, which is maybe twenty-five years later. She blames her brother who wrote the will for gypping her out of her inheritance even though she had sat in the room and had agreed when this was decided."

Lake says that her mother had never worked and "everything she has was given to her by my father." Tina Smith, her daughter believes, felt slighted because she equated the inheritance with a measure of her father's love—a common attitude, experts say. As an adult, Lake has tried to heal the breach between her mother and her uncle. "I was researching our family history one day and discovered that I had an uncle I never knew about. I called him and went to visit him one day with my daughter. We had a delightful time, which I later told my mother about. Since then, she has spoken to him a few times." Although she never discusses her feelings about being cut out of the will, Lake's mother seems willing to let some bygones be bygones. "I was surprised she even talked to him," says Lake.

Without prompting from Lake, her mother and uncle might have taken their estrangement to their graves. Tina Smith's parents thought they were carrying out the very wishes she and Tim Smith had suggested; yet neither generation took into account the deep-seated instincts that children have about equality among siblings. Parents have to understand the nature of sibling rivalry before they make any "powder-keg" decisions with regard to their wealth.

There are so many issues parents have to consider when creating an estate plan. Often, the older generation cares very much about equality, according to Thayer Willis, Licensed Clinical Social Worker and wealth consultant, but even the smallest details about the estate can disproportionately complicate the decisions. Even if you have just stocks and bonds, the quality of these assets could vary and incite arguments about those different values. The situation is further complicated by jewelry, real estate, vacation homes—items with not only monetary worth but also sentimental importance, says Willis. Theoretically, you could be equal in a monetary division of the estate, but leave heirs fighting over the family's silver coffee service.

Because of these potential landmines, Lisa Schneider says, "there are many reasons why parents think about treating children differently, but the majority of the time, they will not act on it. Most of the time they will live with their concerns because they do not want to be perceived as treating any of their children differently." Still, the reality is that some children need to be treated differently with respect to money. There are the obvious reasons, such as mental or physical incapacity that render a child unable to earn a living. Beyond that, there are more subtle differences, not only in that some assets are not neatly divisible but in the ages and levels of responsibility of the children. In fact, parents may discover that by distributing their assets equally, the inheritances are in essence unequal because they are not meeting each child's specific needs. One of the ways to avoid years of misunderstanding and resentment about the way the children were treated is for parents to talk about their intentions for the wealth. As always, when children understand the reasons behind the action, they are more likely to embrace it.

Clarifying Your Intentions

No family wants to come to blows in court over the will, yet that can happen when heirs perceive they've been mistreated and that a sibling was given preference. Experts say much of the strife can be avoided if parents overcome their fear of talking with their offspring before any plan has been put in place. According to Joan DiFuria, parents will find it easier to talk to their children if they do some homework first by asking themselves a critical two-part question: "What is the value of leaving money to a child or grandchild and what do I want to accomplish for that child?"

Aside from the desire to be fair, there are many reasons for parents to communicate to heirs about the estate. If parents have developed a mission statement with their families, they will want to match their estate plan to that mission. In some cases that means giving more to charity. In other instances, it involves coming up with alternative plans for children who have exhibited fiscal irresponsibility. It also might mean skipping over the children, if they have productive and lucrative careers, and providing trusts for the grandchildren. The key, as always, is that parents tell their offspring about their plans to avoid surprises later. Furthermore, they should discuss their plans in a way that incorporates their values and expectations for their children.

If parents plan their estate around money, but don't discuss their values, then the money will likely disappear in a way the parents didn't intend. "No parent or grandparent wants to see money squandered on drugs or alcohol," says DiFuria. "You don't want to encourage a fiscal relationship that takes away from the family relationship." Problems can be sidestepped if parents are clear in their intentions, she asserts. "There is a reality that fair and equal don't go together." She counsels parents to make their decisions value-oriented versus judgment-oriented. "I ask parents, do they want to collude with bad behavior or reward good behavior?" Throughout their children's lives, parents make decisions about their well-being, she says. "Do they have milk today or can they have soda? Can they watch TV before they do their homework?" Decisions about wealth should be no different.

There are factors beyond the child's character, such as age and level of responsibility, that should be considered. Sometimes a child ends up in a bad marriage and the parents don't trust the spouse. Catastrophic health problems could run up huge hospital and rehabilitation debt. Parents have to take everything into account when planning how to leave the money. "Look at who the child is and then look at external factors like productivity, hardships, marriage," says DiFuria. "Parents need to know that it doesn't have to be equal. But they should also realize there is no perfect answer if the bequests are unequal. Kids have calculators on their foreheads and they keep tabs on everything. If there is favoritism, it will be seen in how the parents give the money."

Another benefit of parents communicating their intentions and values early, adds DiFuria, is that it gives children the chance to amend their errant behavior. "Often, they step up to the plate and say, 'I want to be responsible.'"

If the family council is armed with a sound strategy for fiscal education that extends from childhood through adulthood, negligent heirs who decide that it's time to mend their ways and become responsible will have a proven path to follow. Beyond that, children feel a larger sense of belonging to the family and its mission when they have been included in its future planning. Children understand the larger purpose when parents talk about their values instead of just about the money. In families where common values are not embraced by all, DiFuria notes that "forewarned" is also "forearmed" at the reading of the will. If a family member knows about the estate plan beforehand but is still bent on litigation, it will usually come out in the discussions with the parents and they can then stipulate that anyone who contests the will is going to be left with nothing. "It can really make it easier for the other siblings," DiFuria says, because they are the ones who will have to deal with the situation after the parents are gone. This parental control for discouraging future lawsuits is a fairly common tactic—at least among the rich and famous. Clauses that make it difficult to sue force the inheritors to put up [with the plan] and shut up. One of Bing Crosby's sons has talked publicly about the unequal treatment he received in his famous father's will, but added that he knew that if he contested it, he would receive nothing. Although such clauses may coerce children into silently accepting their lot, it doesn't usually do much to enhance family harmony. In fact, it typically intensifies sibling rivalry and causes deeper division in the family between the perceived "haves and have-nots." Better to prepare the family with frequent and open communication through family meetings in the hope that they will understand and embrace all the motives of the estate plan.

Among the biggest fears that wealth generators have are that their children or grandchildren won't understand the value of earning money (as discussed in Chapter 6) or that they are too young to receive an inheritance, and consequently will squander it. Estate planners should not ignore the fact that their younger or less responsible heirs should be treated differently from their older or more dependable siblings. Parents may also recognize that irresponsible heirs may grow into exemplary adults with an increased ability to manage wealth. Estate planning asks parents to predict their own demise, the timing of which is usually out of their control. For all these reasons, trusts are an excellent way to leave money to children who might not be ready to handle it in a constructive way.

Trusts offer flexibility in how they are established, with the creator being able to set standards for distribution based on any number of factors. Distribution amounts and frequency can be adjusted so that the heir doesn't receive a boatload of money all at once. Some experts and parents favor the far end of the control spectrum, the so-called incentive trusts. Parents can put in any provisions they desire for how assets will be distributed, but experts caution that every angle and scenario needs to be forecasted. "I'm a believer in incentive trusts under the right circumstances," says Thayer Willis, because parents can set values that need to be achieved before the trust pays out, for example, a college education. "These trusts work well only in high-functioning emotionally healthy families, in which children know that they are loved no matter what they do."

In a dysfunctional family, the danger is that heirs will probably view incentive trusts as power plays by control-freak parents who won't ever let them live their own lives, or as a lack of trust. "[These trusts] can work," says Willis, "but there has to be unconditional love and support, with a lot of flexibility." Timelines can be corrosive, for example. If an heir must finish school by a certain date in order to inherit, but a health crisis requiring extended hospitalization or rehabilitation prevents that, the trust mustn't be too rigid in its edicts. "The hardest part of incentive trusts is writing them well," cautions Willis. "In fact, relatively few are written because the exercise of getting it right is exhausting. That said, in the strong, positive, healthy family they can provide values, motivators, choices and effective wealth transfer."

Parents say a lot when they establish incentive trusts—about themselves, their desires for their children, and the goals they value. Consequently Lisa Schneider counsels parents to bear in mind all possible scenarios. "What appears to be a good idea on the surface may not be deep down. These need a great deal of thought and analysis." She says parents most often err because of the very reason DiFuria and Willis mention: the measures they use to induce heirs sometimes unintentionally disagree with the values they are trying to instill.

As an example, clients of Schneider's wanted to reward their children for working hard by establishing a trust that would pay out a dollar for every dollar earned by the child. "If your child is a doctor, lawyer, stock broker, or other professional, it can be extremely rewarding. If, however, your child is a teacher, a missionary, poet, or artist, he may work just as hard or harder, but doesn't make as much money," advises Schneider. Are the parents actually rewarding hard work, as they intended, or are they rewarding high incomes?

In this case, intentions do not match the outcome. Another client of Schneider's wanted to set up an incentive trust that paid money for each grandchild born. Does that motivate heirs to propagate? And what about those who are unable to have children? Are they being punished for something that is beyond their control? The incentive also omits provisions for adopted children, raising the question in the children's minds of what the parents ultimately valued. "In some instances incentive trusts work, and in some they don't. Parents have to be careful to determine what to incentivize and how they will measure success," says Schneider.

Even when using trusts to pay out inheritances, parents have to ensure that children are prepared for the wealth, in whatever form it is received. This is especially true if the inheritance doesn't come from the parents and may make only one sibling suddenly wealthy. Willis recounts a client whose story reads like a heart-wrenching fairy tale. She describes a 21-year-old woman who was a "total mess" when she came to her. The client had a twin sister and two younger sisters, all of whom were very close. The family was one of modest means and the parents were divorced. A "mysterious godmother" appeared on the scene only twice in the life of the twins. Apparently, she had once been a close friend of their mother's but the two were now estranged.

When they were 16, the twins received a surprise multimillion-dollar inheritance from the godmother. "At first the whole family was quite delighted, and the twins thought of the inheritance as being for all the girls because they were quite close," says Willis. The twins readily shared the money, buying one sister a car and sending the other one to college. The college-bound sister, however, languished at school, receiving "incompletes" in most of her courses, and the twins wondered why she wasn't taking her education seriously. They expressed doubts about whether the rest of the family valued their gifts, with the result that "psychologically, they became separated from the family because they were in the position of bene- factors," says Willis.

Willis adds that by the time the family came to her, "they were at each others' throats. It was a heartbreaking example of what an unexpected inheritance can do, and it was *so* unequal compared to what the younger sisters could ever expect." The twin who first came to see Willis was "so crushed by what she thought was the loss of her family." After three or four years, she was able to reconnect with them again, but she found further evidence of the lengths to which parents will sometimes go in order to make their children feel equal. One day, while exploring in the attic of her family home, she came across a box filled with unopened Christmas and birthday gifts from the godmother. Her mother explained that she didn't think it was right to give her those gifts because they were undoubtedly very expensive and beyond the means of what the parents could afford to give the other girls. The moral of the story, says Willis, is that parents need to educate children about money so they will be prepared to handle it, no matter what its source may be. The family also clearly never hashed out their values concerning money, either before or after the inheritance—a situation that leads to dysfunction, as we have seen time and time again.

Regular family meetings to develop a list of common values and a mission statement after the twins inherited the money might have helped the family understand how it could further the goals of each of its members as well as the family as a whole. A common mission based on core family values would have saved the heartache of the twins being put in the awkward position of sole guardians of the money and their windfall could have enriched everyone. Instead, the money had a different meaning for each individual, erroneous judgments were made regarding the motives for the spending, and misunderstandings remained unresolved.

We'll say it again: educating children when they are young will go a long way toward establishing success in adulthood. Tell children about money, but combine it with a good fiscal education. This is preventive medicine for so many of the ills that parents hear about in other wealthy families. Thayer Willis adds that parents should tell adult children as much as they feel they can about their estates so the children can do their own planning with their parents' blessing. As we learned from the stories in Chapter 6, talking about money should not be taboo. "Sometimes [heirs] are told that nothing is coming to them, when in fact they are getting an inheritance. I've had clients who have spent their lives working in careers they hate because they thought they had to make a lot of money for retirement. They end up feeling resentful."

Parents who fear that telling children about an inheritance will turn into what Willis calls "a disincentive problem" have an antidote. She advises them to teach the children about all aspects of handling money, beginning when they are young (for example, Joline Godfrey's curriculum as outlined in Chapter 6). "People often wonder why wealthy children need to learn budgeting, but by teaching them sound realistic financial principles like avoiding debt, keeping a ledger, saving, investing, and earning, they learn so much more. Building that foundation is the single most important thing parents can do. Whether the goal is to be equal or fair, the next generation should be financially literate," says Willis.

Parents find that as they teach children the basics of handling money, the fears of mismanagement slip away. When children are young, begin to teach the value of money by instituting Rockefeller's one-third rule; for example, allocate one-third to savings, one-third to charity, and one-third for spending. As children get older, they can learn to adhere to a budget and later to manage a checking account or a credit card. By mastering the simple concepts along the way, children develop into mature money managers, they will be less likely to view an inheritance as a windfall for spending, and parents will feel more comfortable giving them the money.

By imparting values around simple money management, parents endow their children with a sense of stewardship. DiFuria says she sees parents choosing to disclose their plans and values with the next generation more often than they did a generation ago. "More and more we see parents making their intentions clear, because they're not as afraid of the ramifications, and there are people to help." Education won't provide all the answers for parents, but there are additional techniques for ensuring that their wishes are carried out. Let's look at trusts and how to plan for the nonmonetary mementos that every family cherishes.

Structuring the Bequests

Sometimes, even after providing a good fiscal education to their heirs, parents don't trust a child's spouse or they see children who won't loosen their grip on the "easy come, easy go" attitude toward money. The parents still want to appear to treat heirs fairly, but are afraid of doing more damage to the next generation by letting them squander the fortune.

Parents who don't want to risk the unintended consequences of incentive trusts, or who don't want to exert that much control, might consider some of the more straightforward methods. Testamentary (created by will) or intervivos (created during life) trusts for the benefit of children and grandchildren can provide some peace of mind for the person establishing the trust while protecting the heirs from their own bad decisions as well as from creditors and spousal claims.

Such trusts can provide a regular income (not protected from the claims of others) yet keep the principal safe from claims. A trustee will make discretionary decisions regarding distributions. Schneider advises parents to appoint independent or corporate trustees rather than members of the family. Making a family member into his "brother's keeper" will only incite conflict, she warns. A trustee who is responsible for distributions based on certain criteria may have more flexibility in meeting the unanticipated needs of the heirs yet still keep to the core values of the parents. For example, the trust may pay all the education expenses for a child and the down payment on his first home or business. The parents are saying, in essence, that they value education and want to help their children start their adult lives, but are refusing to fund the child's every whim or imposing values that heirs may find restricting.

Trusts are favored ways to leave inheritances, because they can save on certain inheritance taxes and enable parents to decide when their children will be mature enough to receive money and the amount of that inheritance. When used in this way, trusts can effectively disguise the motivations of parents who want to treat their children fairly but have doubts about a child's ability to handle an inheritance. For example, one of Schneider's clients wanted to leave money to his four sons, all of whom were doing well. One son, however, had problems with creditors related to his marriage. The client wanted to leave money in trust to that son but didn't want him to know he was being treated differently than the other three. Schneider's solution was to set up a trust for each son, all having the same terms of distribution and principle protection. The three sons without creditor problems have children, so their trusts were set up as generation-skipping trusts. That gave the sons the benefit of income while the principal was protected for the grandchildren. There was no inheritance tax imposed on the principal for the children (the trust principal was "skipping" a generation and passing on to the grandchildren). The son with the creditor issues, who does not have children, has the same provisions in his trust—income distribution only, with the principal protected. In essence, all four sons were treated the same, but the motivation for setting up the trusts was different. For the son with problems, his principal is protected from his spouse and from creditors. In the case of the other three sons, the principal is protected and allowed to grow without certain taxes for their children.

DiFuria agrees that trusts are appropriate vehicles for children and grandchildren who are irresponsible with money and adds that the key to making any trust work is to discuss with children why the trust is being set up and using the discussion as an opportunity to pass along values concerning wealth. If a child becomes upset about her treatment, the parent has the opportunity to talk to her and allow her to step up to the plate. It won't be easy, says DiFuria, "I've never seen kids who are irresponsible say its fair if the responsible child gets more."

One other type of trust should be mentioned. For all the potential battles that might be anticipated, it's rare that siblings balk at extraordinary financial treatment for special-needs children who will never be able to earn their own living because of mental or physical limitations. The challenge for parents in these instances is ensuring that they've taken care of the child when they won't be around. Special needs trusts should be established in a way that doesn't preclude the child from receiving federal or state benefits. "Once deceased, parents have no legal obligation to support their [special-needs] children, but they do have the ability to provide for their luxuries over and above what public benefits cover," says Lisa Schneider. Parents of disabled or special-needs children have to consider who will care for them, in what environment, and whether their needs are greater than those of their other children, says Schneider.

Other ways to protect beneficiaries include a college savings account for minor beneficiaries, to be used for higher education expenses. However, parents might want to steer clear of Uniform Gift to Minor Accounts (UGMA) or Uniform Transfer to Minor Accounts (UTMA) because these usually pay out at the age of majority, when the beneficiaries can spend them any way they choose. The age of majority is determined by each state's statute, but generally it's 18 or 21. Often these accounts are set up at the time of the birth of a child or grandchild and if substantial yearly gifts are made, the distribution amount is beyond what most account creators envision. The child merely has to show proof of age to take out the entire amount. "All at once, a Maserati looks pretty good," says Schneider.

Even in the most buttoned-up estate plans, there are still the items that can't be assigned a monetary value, and it's difficult to be fair if more than one child attaches special meaning to a particular heirloom. Schneider says there are a few ways to handle the family assets that have more sentimental than economic value. Assigning a dollar amount doesn't account for the real worth of the item. "How does one place a value on mother's antique cookie jars or the family photo album?" The best option, Schneider adds, is to reach agreement while the parents are still alive about who receives the silver service and who takes the diamond earrings.

Even so, parents can hit an unexpected snag when they ask their children to identify what assets they want after Mom and Dad are gone. "What I see more often than not is that children don't want to discuss it," says Schneider. "It's almost as if they're telling the parents they don't want them around." If the children won't decide, the parents have to do it for them, says Schneider, or they have to devise a system where the children are forced to choose among the heirlooms. If the parents decide to make the decision alone, one option is to write a side letter to the will, explaining why they gave certain items to particular children and reinforcing that they love all equally. If they want the children to retain choice, they could use the "longest straw" method of deciding who goes first, second, and so on, using a round-robin approach to selecting the valuables.

As a last resort, a corporate trustee, who is removed from the family sentimentality, can make the decision. That method is not only impersonal, but the trustee is likely to try to assign value to the items, which does not take into account its real meaning to the heirs. Communication with heirs can go a long way toward helping them understand their parents' intentions for the wealth and for special items of sentimental value. When talking doesn't work, however, there are structures that will provide the appearance of fairness while protecting the heirs from themselves and from the claims of others.

In the next chapter, we give the dilemma a twist by examining what happens when parents don't intend to leave much of an inheritance to the children, but instead seek to create a legacy through charitable endeavors. Once again, when parents don't take the time to explain their dreams and wishes, the next generation might assume the worst.

Chapter Eight

Strategic
Philanthropy

THE DILEMMA:

I want to give some of my wealth back to society, but how can I do it without my children thinking I've given away their inheritance, and in a manner that will reflect our values and enhance the family legacy?

A CHARITABLE LEGACY that endures beyond your children and your children's children requires strategic planning around the family's values and ultimately carrying out the portion of the family mission statement that expresses its desire to return some of its riches to humanity.

Later in life, founders often enter a reflective period during which they seek to donate to various institutions or charitable endeavors in return for the opportunities they received. The list of possible recipients is as long as the founder's dreams—a university, a scholarship endowment, a public library, an organization that helps disadvantaged youth, and many others. As we'll see later in this chapter, it is sometimes the children who have philanthropic tendencies and seek to carry out what they believe were the founder's legacies.

The tension inherent in the dilemma of donating to philanthropy is that although the founder has the fortune to "repay" society, he wants to avoid potential conflict in the family by dipping into the pot that heirs believe belongs to them. Understanding the correlation between love and inheritance, the founder hopes his children will see the same positive benefit to charitable giving that he embraces. Chances are good the children will support the founder's passion for a legacy, but not if they are caught by surprise.

In Chapter 7, we looked at fairness to the next generation in estate planning. In the first part of this chapter, charity essentially becomes the favored child and parents must be just as cautious in their approach to heirs who may not share their charitable passions and believe the money should come to them, not to an "outsider."

Before the founder can move forward with his plans, he has to set the stage for the next generation through education and communication so that they understand and support the commitment. Otherwise, the family and heirs feel cut out of the decision—and out of the will. Misguided assumptions on the part of both generations will bury any chance of clear and open communication.

Once the plans have been clarified, and the family endorses the charitable enterprise, the next step entails learning the difference between simply writing a check and giving strategically. The latter involves more of a commitment but pays back the giver by providing a fuller sense of the experience. Families may want to go so far as to establish a foundation, requiring a committee or family council to handle administrative duties and possibly to mentor the next generation in business and charitable principles. The benefit of the foundation is that it gives structure to the philanthropy and offers an opportunity to bring the younger generations into the fold and teach them firsthand the family's values and mission. In this chapter we'll examine the following issues:

- *Avoiding communication:* The effect of not talking about philanthropic legacies can lead to bitterness.
- *Educating the next generation:* When children understand the charitable intentions they are more likely to embrace them.
- *Becoming strategic:* An approach that blends a monetary gift

with personal involvement brings greater rewards to the giver.
- *Choosing an approach:* There are many different areas and methods for charitable giving, depending on the donor's interests.

When families unite around a founder's belief in philanthropy, the legacies they create can reap enormous rewards for the entire family for several generations. Third and fourth generations speak with pride about the charitable endeavors of their forebears. During the industrialist years before the turn of the twentieth century, empire builders such as Whitney, Frick, Vanderbilt, Bessemer, and Carnegie shaped the country's destiny. The museums, schools, libraries, and foundations they established continue to enrich us almost a century later.

Scotsman Andrew Carnegie stands apart in his dedication to charitable endeavors. Early in his career, Carnegie knew he would one day convert his zest for capitalism into gifts that the people could share regardless of their personal means. Believing that "a rich man who dies rich dies in disgrace," Carnegie manifested his conviction after he sold his company in 1901. He put a large amount of his wealth into financing future endowments and in 1911 he funded The Carnegie Corporation. Through his gifts, Carnegie established the free public library system, with some 3,000 libraries built worldwide, along with Carnegie-Mellon University in Pittsburgh and Carnegie Hall in New York City. His endowments are so entrenched in our society that preschoolers throughout the world watch their beloved *Sesame Street,* unaware that the popular educational children's show is funded by money originating from the steel industrialist.

None of Andrew Carnegie's fifty or so descendents inherited vast amounts of capital, but his legacy is rich in philanthropic culture. Families who follow his example are hoping to provide future generations with a similar connection to the founders and their mission. The challenge is to do it in a way that the entire family embraces with pride of ownership.

Avoiding Communication

The effect of not talking about philanthropic intentions can lead to bitterness. Sound familiar? Communication early and often is the key to at least reducing the potential for strife over family issues, including how the wealth is transferred. Consistent discussion about the estate plan enables the next generation to feel they are a part of the decision, thus making them more likely to accept it. When philanthropy comes as a surprise, the founder has to work harder to overcome his offspring's negative reaction. He has to wait for the possibility that the next generation will reach the age when they themselves understand the concept of giving back. Such was the case in the Liautaud family introduced in Chapter 1.

The Liautaud Graduate School of Business at the University of Illinois in Chicago stands as a proud testament to a man who embodied America's can-do spirit. Father of the clan, Jim Liautaud, founded a technology firm soon after he graduated college. His son, Jimmy John Liautaud, followed in his entrepreneurial footsteps and began a successful chain of gourmet sandwich shops. When Jim, his wife, Gina, and Jimmy John Liautaud endowed the university with a financial gift to establish the Business School, they did it as a united trio. Privately, however, the gift to the university caused a rift in the family that was only recently mended.

When Jim Liautaud first talked about the gift, it was as a done deal. "I was caught completely off guard," recalls Jimmy John Liautaud. "I felt wronged," as if his father was giving away his rightful inheritance. "Somebody else was getting the mother lode." Once he realized the gift was going to happen regardless of his personal opposition, he capitulated and added some of his own money. Jimmy John Liautaud changed his attitude toward his father's beneficence, in part because the train was out of the station, so to speak, and in part because as he himself neared the age of 40, he'd come to understand his father's motives. "I'm in a different place now than I was a few years ago," he says. He now understands that there are different stages in life. His feelings about his father and his motives have matured. At first, his reaction was "not only is he kicking us out of the nest, he's taking our dough and giving it to someone else and we're saying, 'hey, wait, what about us; we're trying to build our own nests?'" Describing himself as "needy" in his 20s and 30s, his viewpoint at 40 is "much less judgmental. I worked hard, and I'm now wealthy in my own right."

Jim Liautaud admits that his second-oldest child was initially against the gift to the university, "for reasons that escape me now." He adds that "today, he is a big supporter and the other kids are all quite proud of the gift and feel it will have a permanent effect on their lives." In years to come, Liautaud descendants will be able to look on the school with pride of ownership and the miscommunication will have been buried with the current generation.

In other families, the negative repercussions will have lasting effects and will become part of the legacy. Parents who view the fortune they made as not belonging to the family, and who make decisions based solely on their own wishes, may get more than they bargained for. In the retelling by the heirs, the family narrative can become tainted by lingering resentment.

Lee Hausner has counseled several families where she has witnessed bitterness among beneficiaries because the amount that was given to charity was significant, while their inheritances were relatively modest. To add insult to injury, she says, they were then expected to give their time and energy as members of the foundation board. Being equitable with the children, and including open communication as part of the plan, will help ward off strife over the legacy. "Although massive inheritances are often not in the best interest of beneficiaries, there should be some reasonable balance between personal inheritance and the philanthropic initiative of the senior generation," Hausner says. "Good communication will do much to arrive at the best balance." It will also stave off resentment that can lead children to plot the destruction of their parents' intent. Joan DiFuria echoes the view of Jay Hughes when she says that if the next generation doesn't have an understanding of why their parents made the decision to leave money to charity, they will do what they can to prevent those gifts from being made once the parents are gone. "People want to take care of themselves first, then their

loved ones, and then third is charity," she says. That is precisely why
it is so important for a founder to understand that the entire family
has to support his vision for a legacy because they can continue to
strengthen it through the ages.

Sometimes parents communicate, but not enough, DiFuria
notes. This also leads to a breakdown in the family. "They say, 'we're
giving you this amount, and the rest is going to charity' and the kids
don't know if the rest is 100 percent more than they've gotten."
Communicating clearly, completely, and consistently will assist heirs
in understanding the legacy. Along with communication, it is important to educate heirs about philanthropy and allow them to enjoy the
benefits firsthand. This will broaden their acceptance. The fullness
of the approach will take hold when children come into their own,
ingrained with the values and preparation for the family's legacy.

Educating the Next Generation

Educating children about the family's values around philanthropy
(best done during family meetings that begin when the children are
young, as discussed in Part II) means there will be no bombshells
and resentment later, and children will be more likely to embrace
their parents' wishes. Parents find that they not only ease their
guilt about estate planning decisions, but also the children reap the
benefits of charitable intentions that go far beyond just giving away
money. The often unspoken message is that children should not be
dependent on an inheritance and it forces them to earn a living, the
benefits of which are great in terms of self-esteem.

When her two children were young, Jean Herrera (not her real
name) says that she and her husband wanted to instill in them "the
importance of finding their own way in life and not being dependent
on the family for an income for life." By involving them in philanthropy, they also taught the children to pay attention to those who
are not so blessed.

Although the children were aware of the family's wealth, the
couple tried to shield them from excess. To that end, they stepped
up their charitable giving. In the late 1990s, shortly after they sold

the businesses, they enlisted the children's help in setting up a foundation.

Caring for the less fortunate was a lesson Herrera had always taught her children, even before they had the wealth from the sale of the family business. Every year they adopted a family at Thanksgiving. "As they got older, we put them in charge of things," says Herrera. The children were to call the needy family to find out what they needed for the holiday. Then, working with a budget, they bought food and gifts for the family. "We gave them no input at all. They've done that since they were little," she says.

The children were homeschooled for a year while the family lived in Spain and they volunteered for some kind of community service every week. "They've always grown up with the belief that you give back to those who are less fortunate. I don't think they've connected that with having money," Herrera says. "They know we're not planning to make them wealthy."

Herrera's daughter Sarah, now in graduate school, says that working with her family's foundation has taught her "there are people out there who really need it. I've had a really easy life." She tithes to the family foundation, a task she finds difficult ("I try to write the check before I think about it") and is able to direct where she wants her money spent. "If I want to save the money and do something with greater impact, I can do that, or I can do smaller things."

Sarah Herrera says, "For the most part, I don't have a sense of entitlement for my parent's money. If every penny they had went to charity, I'd probably be a little disappointed, but if more money goes to the foundation than to me, I'm OK with that."

Her philanthropic viewpoint, gleaned through her parents' actions as well as her own involvement, has made philanthropy an integral part of Sarah's life. She understands that her parents want her to have the value of earning her own living instead of living off an inheritance. She finds it laudable that she learned this value early.

The age at which philanthropy is taught is up to the parents and the instruction can take on many forms. As Thayer Willis learned, one of the most effective methods for teaching philanthropy is to involve the entire family in a dedicated charitable effort, involving both time and money, so they can learn from one another. When Willis and her husband began an annual tradition of philanthropy, they intended to teach their two children solid lessons about giving. In the end, they were astonished at how much they themselves had learned as parents. Practicing what you preach as parents provides a lesson like no other. Simple yet innovative ways to involve the family in charitable giving will provide a meaningful manifestation of the family's stated mission.

Willis says both she and her husband grew up without a family forum for philanthropy. Willis is an heir to the Georgia-Pacific Company and says that although her parents gave to charity individually, the children were not included. "We were always considered to be children, even when we were adults," she says, "and not competent enough to be included in any decisions. I was brought up by parents who believed that we should be kept in the dark about wealth and even about finances to a great extent. We were given money when we needed it."

Willis contends, "Family philanthropy provides a tremendous opportunity to teach financial literacy. It's a natural." She and her husband viewed the lack of philanthropy in their backgrounds as the stimulus to create their own legacy with their children. When their children were 8 and 12 years old, the Willises came up with their model, and selected January 1st as the start date. Willis suggests that for tax reasons, it may make sense to start at Thanksgiving, for example, to meet the end of the year tax deadline. "We didn't have a New Year's tradition, our children are young and the amount of money is small, so for now, this is a good way to start the year. In fact, changing the starting date later, if we use larger amounts of money could, in itself, be a great lead-in to tax education."

Each member of the family, including Willis's mother, receives the same dollar amount and decides how to distribute it. The amount can be divided into three parts with one part going to the giver's first-choice charity or cause. The other two parts can go to the chosen charities of the others, which encourages family members to "sell" their charitable ideas to the family.

The Willis family sets a date to meet for the purpose of discussing their choices. Willis says this model helps families avoid messy misunderstandings when the kids are older. "If you do this, then the younger family members have experience in working as a team and understanding their own and their family's values, and all that gets talked about," she says. "It gets around the suspicion of the young adults thinking the parents are giving away their inheritance."

Willis says children don't have to be given a lot of money to understand the concept. "Our kids love it; they just jumped right in. They thought the amount was a lot of money, so they took it very seriously." Clay, who was only 8 when they began the program, decided that children in the world should not have to be hungry and decided to give to the Oregon Food Bank. "I helped him with his research, but I let him lead the way," says Willis. The lesson was further reinforced when his class took a field trip to the same food bank where he had donated his money. "They filled bags with the ingredients for a potato casserole for 5,000 recipients," according to Willis. "He got to work for a day where he donated," she says. "What a great gift." Willis adds that this family philanthropy model can be expanded in many ways; volunteering at the chosen charity will likely be an important component.

In addition to children's hunger, Clay Willis focused on children in hospitals. He wanted to enable parents and siblings to be nearby at a time when a child might be frightened. "So he designated some of his money for the Ronald McDonald House Charities," says Willis. "Again, he was able to research this on the Internet with my help."

Willis's preteen daughter, Julianne, was confident about conducting her own research, and chose health and education in Armenia. "We said, 'Really? How did you choose that?'" says Willis. World Vision had visited their church, and her daughter surfed the Internet to find the organization's website and drew her own conclusions. "She learned that when you're poor in a developing country it's worse than being poor in the United States because of the lack of resources [available in those countries]. She decided to give to health and education because if you can get healthy, you can get an education; and if you can do that, you can get a job."

Willis says that the family will continue to reap the intangible benefits of their charitable giving tradition. "One of the best parts [of our program] was seeing how competent our children are at identifying their values and extending those values into the world. My husband and I were really surprised at how well it worked. We saw qualities in the children that we never saw before," she says. "I hope I'm conveying our awe at how well they did." Willis's experience suggests an important aspect of giving, namely, that it's not always just about the money, as we see next.

Becoming Strategic

An approach that blends a monetary gift with personal involvement brings greater rewards to the giver. As Willis teaches her children that it feels good to give back, she is also teaching them to be strategic. By researching their gifts to find what coincides with their personal values, explaining the importance of what they are doing to the family, and following the monetary commitment with the gift of personal interaction, they learn to understand and appreciate the results of what they are doing.

Time or money devoted to philanthropy can return enormous value. But all too often, donors contribute passively by writing a few checks to various organizations, often from a sense of obligation or as a result of pressure instead of a true passion for a cause. Strategic philanthropy entails purposeful giving through a commitment to investigate and monitor charities and to decide which resources will be most valuable for both the charity and the benefactor.

When families make decisions about their philanthropic values and mission, they experience the fullness of giving that enriches their souls and they pass their charitable intentions on to the next generation. Whether giving multimillions of dollars or much smaller amounts, donors gain satisfaction from giving when they follow their monetary commitment with a personal one.

In 2004, the Salvation Army, an organization known for providing food and addiction recovery assistance, received the largest private gift from a single individual in memory. Joan Kroc, widow of Ray

Kroc, the founder of the ubiquitous restaurant chain McDonald's, endowed the organization in her will. Established as a means to provide "soup, soap, and salvation," the Salvation Army used the Kroc windfall to open more of the community centers that Joan Kroc had visited and admired. A previous gift had been earmarked for such a center in San Diego. The center features swimming pools, basketball courts, an ice rink, and an arts arena. Half of the Kroc endowment was directed toward opening new centers and the other half was for operating revenue. The Salvation Army would still have to raise additional funds, but Kroc's seed money meant the difference between a vision and actual bricks and mortar. The Salvation Army was not the only group to benefit from Joan Kroc's largesse. She also reportedly gave money to National Public Radio and the Ronald McDonald House Charities. Clearly, Kroc's involvement with specific charities was targeted, personal, and in keeping with a long tradition of support. Ray Kroc had been a bell ringer at a Salvation Army collection kettle in the 1950s.

Ask any significant donor who understands the concept of strategic giving to explain the reasons behind an endowment and listen to what they say. Benefactors like Kroc, the Liautauds, the Herreras, and the Willises convey enthusiasm for their investment in philanthropy. This is because they have given fully, whether they established a long-lasting legacy, like Jim Liautaud, or have seen the difference even a small commitment can make, like young Clay Willis.

Jim Liautaud says he focuses his charitable donations in two areas. He has been a long-time supporter of his alma mater, the University of Illinois, specifically through his involvement in its entrepreneur program. He founded and funded the university's Family Business Council and in November 2003 made the substantial gift to the business school. His wife, Gina, is president of Lithuanian Children's Hope, a project she founded a decade ago to provide training for surgeons to aid Lithuanian children. Despite the fact that the business school at the University of Illinois bears his name, Liautaud says his charitable intentions are about more than bricks and mortar. "I invest only in fluid and soulful directions, with all my money focused on people and ideas, never names on buildings."

Jimmy John Liautaud has a somewhat less focused approach, but is still strategic and thoughtful. "It makes me feel good." He has a screening system for requests, which he claims "takes the heat off." Applicants are asked to write a letter and to meet certain criteria before being considered. "We do what's dear to us," he says, citing the YMCA, a wildlife organization, and his contributions to his parents' causes. Families can adopt a strategic approach to philanthropy at any time in their narrative. Often it's not the founder's legacy that is being carried out, but someone in a later generation who inspires others in the family to give, as we see next.

Enticing the family to participate in a philanthropic plan doesn't have to come from the wealth originator. Amy Welsh (not her real name), part of the third generation of a wealthy family, grew up privileged and her munificence began to surface while she was in her teens. "I had a social conscience from a young age and this was a way for me to balance the privilege that I enjoyed and my gratitude for it." She calls herself a philanthropic activist and has been at it for nearly twenty years. She and her spouse first began giving in the late 1980s and says that she was "tactically inspired," during the decade-long rise in the stock market that followed. She established a donor-advised fund—a tax-advantaged method set up through a public foundation—where she parked the gains from her stocks while at the same time reducing taxable capital gains.

Welsh didn't get her philanthropic leanings from her parents, even though they regularly gave to charity. Her parents weren't strategic in their giving and, in any case, didn't share their plan with the children. "They had a separate checking account out of which they made their donations; and they gave according to what served their peers," says Welsh. "I don't think they went beyond the obligatory giving of their social group. So it was to the schools we attended, the hospitals that served our family, the garden club—there was no philanthropic plan."

After Welsh's father died and their mother became seriously ill in the early 1990s, she and her three siblings decided to continue giving on their mother's behalf, initially for tax reasons. They established a donor-advised fund. "It made sense," says Welsh. "She got sick, and we were watching the stock market go bananas, so it was a smart estate-planning and tax strategy to put appreciated stock in the fund." The siblings made an effort to give as their mother might have. "We didn't change the essence or the organizations, but we were able to discuss as a family what she might have cared about but didn't know about." For example, they gave a large one-time gift to the Audubon Society and to a natural history museum. "I don't know if my mother would have done that, but we were able to make a decision about a plan, and this gave us a medium for having discussions."

Like many families who begin philanthropy as a way to save taxes, the experience leads to giving for the sake of giving and as a way to get to know one another on a deeper level. Welsh and her siblings decided to expand on their individual philanthropic objectives by allocating an amount to each sibling out of their mother's donor-advised fund. A year later, they brought in the next generation and gave them smaller amounts to direct to the charities of their choice. Each member of the family was responsible for reporting on the results of their gifts at an annual family meeting, and if they didn't make their gift within the year, they lost it.

"We had about five years where our generation and the next generation were able to share our passions and concern about the world using the money in the donor-advised fund," Welsh recalls. "We used it as a vehicle for communication as well as for philanthropy. It was a way to get to know aspects of each other we wouldn't otherwise have known." In the end, it became too difficult for the family to give together. In 2003 they split the donor-advised fund four ways, with each sibling opening a separate fund. "We realized we're not cut out to do this together," Welsh says. "We were not primed by my parents, and it was too difficult for us to work together."

Still, Welsh cherishes what the family learned about the value of strategic philanthropy, whether they do it together or separately. "Writing a check can provide fleeting gratification, but you're a better philanthropist if you understand what you're doing. Getting involved is a way of being 'fed' in return for the time or money or both that you put into an organization."

As Welsh discovered, families don't have to remain united in their approach to charity. Herrera taught her children young and they are still involved in the family foundation. Her aim was to inspire them to philanthropy, not necessarily impose her own charitable intentions. As they grow older, they may decide to give in an entirely new direction.

Like Welsh, Willis is finding that practicing as a family means the individuals learn from one another, but each is required to research his own charity. This sense of individuality in the midst of working as a team can help families gain maturity because they grow apart and together at the same time—learning to be confident in their own abilities while learning to function as a unit.

Teamwork in families, as we saw in Part I with family businesses, is a precursor to multigenerational development. Just as the family needs its own mission statement, developed with everyone's input, to guide them in living their values, a philanthropic initiative should begin with the same premise. A strategic program begins with a mission statement, or statement of purpose, to outline the philanthropic values and commitment of the donor. It might be as simple as "I support the efforts of education, particularly for those with learning disabilities." Another, more specific, mission statement might read as follows: "The family makes grants based on the values of compassion, love, and service. We support projects of nonprofit organizations that help low-income individuals achieve self-sufficiency, especially women and families. In this way we hope to improve our communities and ultimately the world around us." With a stated purpose, it becomes easier to decide the amount of financial resources or time to commit and which charities to support. If the charities are local, visit them to see the work they're doing and if that supports the stated mission.

Establish the philanthropic mission statement with input from each family member. It should contain specific information concerning its funding policies and how interested parties can apply for a grant. Included in the funding policies are the programs of particular interest to the family, which provide substance to their mission statement, such as the following:

- Women and families, including programs that promote independence, empowerment, and domestic violence education.
- Education, such as child mentoring and after-school programs.
- Job training for those in need.
- Seed money for charities to develop marketing materials and grant-writing designed to secure additional funding.

The family might also list its funding priorities, such as:

- Programs that the family is actively involved in.
- Programs that promote independence and self-sustainability.
- Programs that have a positive effect on the family unit.

The family may take it a step further by specifying what they will not support financially, including ongoing operating expenses, deficits, fund-raisers, repayment of loans, endowments, scholarships, capital campaigns, annual or ongoing campaigns, or direct support for individuals. Once again, mission statements don't have to be as detailed as this, but they should clearly outline the family's values in terms of what they will and will not support. In the previous example, the family chose to exemplify their mission and values regarding philanthropy by actively volunteering in the charities they support financially. The time spent with the charities gives the family a fuller understanding of the needs of each organization and completes its strategic plan. We'll take a look at another example of a family foundation's mission statement later in this chapter.

Choosing an Approach

Once families decide whether to give time, money, or both, they need to examine the various financial charitable vehicles to find the one that best suits its resources and tax situation. Some donors prefer to give during their lifetime, when they can witness the positive effect of their gifts. Others, as part of estate planning, bestow gifts at death through a will or trust. Still others, like Welsh, say they will do both. "We're not waiting to die to give. If someone needs college tuition now, we give it."

An outright contribution—simply cutting a check—is a common form of giving, but be aware of several pitfalls. Check out the organization first for its tax status. Look for 501(c)(3) tax exempt organizations or qualified public charities. To investigate the integrity of larger organizations, two websites provide useful information. They are the American Institute of Philanthropy's rating guide (www.charitywatch.org) and the Better Business Bureau's Wise Giving Alliance (www.give.org). For smaller organizations, ask questions that include who they are, what they do, their fund-raising expenses, short- and long-term goals, and history of donations. Verify their status with the IRS or the local Better Business Bureau and ask for a copy of their annual report.

Another way to give is through giving circles, which are groups of donors with common interests—family members, friends, or like-minded people in the community. Contributions are pooled and administrative tasks are assigned. Some members may conduct on-site visits, others may be responsible for accounting, and still others for monitoring the progress of the chosen charity.

Donor-advised funds provide a tax-advantaged method of giving, with flexibility to direct the distribution of the investment, without taking on the administrative hassles. This is the method Amy Welsh prefers. During the stock market boom of the 1990s, she pulled profits from her investments and parked them in a donor-advised fund until she knew specifically where to allocate the money. Donors give a minimum amount to the public foundation, which takes care of paperwork. Fees are typically in the range of 1 to 5 percent. Donors then have some flexibility in where to direct funds and they receive an immediate income tax deduction for the amount of their gift. If the gift is appreciated stock, donors avoid capital gains tax and also remove the asset from their estate, thus saving estate taxes.

Private or family foundations are usually controlled by an individual or family and make grants to other tax-exempt organizations to carry out their charitable intentions. They are typically formed with an endowment or regular contributions, and the IRS requires

a minimum annual payout. Many families who establish a foundation find it a beneficial way to bring in subsequent generations and
teach them about the family's philanthropic goals and stewardship
of family wealth.

Other planned-giving vehicles include enterprises that involve the
commitment of a gift during life or at death, such as various charitable trusts and bequests through a will. Benefactors are also expanding
their strategy beyond traditional means to include the use of equity
investments or loans. It's a good idea to talk with advisers about any
charitable strategies and it's essential for any nontraditional methods
that are being considered. Strategic philanthropy takes more time
and effort than simply mailing a check, but as Welsh says, "I receive
so much from my involvement. It makes it all much more human."

Some families prefer to have greater control over their charitable
investments. A closer look at family foundations reveals that families
can benefit in two ways. The foundations set some structure for their
charitable plans while at the same time establishing an educational
tool for subsequent generations to learn stewardship. Family foundations allow donors complete control over investments and grantmaking, unlike donor-advised funds, which have some limitations.
The family foundation board has full fiduciary responsibility and
must handle all administration. Experts say they should be funded
with an amount that justifies the operating expenses. Foundations
can be the means for carrying out the family's wishes for generations, but the tradeoff is the monitoring and maintenance required.
Family foundations are a tremendous way for the wealthy to instill
their charitable legacy in future generations while simultaneously
not leaving excessive amounts to heirs.

After Ellen Remmer's father died, she and her family sold his
business and began talking about what to do with their newfound
wealth. They had already decided to establish a new business enterprise, but they wanted to do more. "A couple of us felt that what was
missing from our talks was a social impact for the money." Remmer,
her two sisters, and her mother created a family foundation to assist
disadvantaged girls. In addition to being trustee of her own family
foundation, Remmer is vice president of The Philanthropic Initiative

(TPI), where she assists clients in developing or retooling their philanthropic missions. She says that organized philanthropy has been an optimal way to pass along those values to the next generation.

Remmer and her siblings grew up observing their parents' largesse. "My parents had strong loyalties to institutions and they were generous." Both had been scholarship students and they gave back to their colleges. In addition, her mother was a member of the Junior League and involved in community charities. They participated in a way that Remmer says was "typical of their generation." The inherent message to the children was "that's just part of what you did. We were raised with role models."

Her mother continued throughout her life to be a role model by providing seed money for individual donor-advised funds for each of the children and grandchildren. Remmer says that individual giving opportunities blend well with family charitable structures, because family members can fulfill their own passions separate from the family's philanthropic mission.

When they decided to organize their giving as a family several years ago, Remmer's mother and her two sisters decided on a family foundation for two reasons. They had explored other options, such as community foundations, but because they all lived in different states, they found it hard to decide on one community. There also were not as many charitable vehicles as there are today. The second reason is that a foundation provides a structure for giving. According to Remmer, "there is a seriousness about institutionalizing it as a foundation. There is a certain stature and discipline with required payouts."

The family, however, was not in complete agreement about starting a foundation. Remmer says that funding it in a tax-efficient manner with appreciated company stock, and agreeing to start small, helped everyone feel more at ease. As noted earlier, this is a typical way for families to consider charity. Later, though, it often grows with the family's excitement as they witness the difference their giving makes. Remmer's family foundation was seeded with an amount from the family and Remmer's mother recently left another sizeable donation in her will.

An added benefit of a foundation is that families sometimes find that organizing themselves around a mutual passion makes working together an enjoyable and personally rewarding experience. When created by the second generation, as in the Remmer family, the foundation becomes "theirs" as opposed to a fully formed organization handed down from the founder.

When families like the Remmers are dealing with the complexities embedded in an inherited family business, a foundation devoted to their interests can be an antidote. Remmer says her family foundation's small group of trustees "was just this wonderful cocoon." She adds that the foundation provided them with "a healing process" after difficulties they encountered with the sale of their family business, when they had to learn to work together as a family without a strong patriarch as their anchor.

The caveat to the closeness the foundation enjoys is that they know that it will be short-lived and will require more structure as the next generation matures. "We are a typical first-generation foundation, with almost no policies and procedures," Remmer wryly notes. "Most first generations know and trust each other innately, and there is a greater sense of shared values." In Remmer's own experience, she and her siblings had to overcome only a few personality quirks. She, for instance, had to realize that as a consultant, she was trying to conduct foundation business in a formal manner with a lot of forms, while the others thought she was going overboard. Today, the foundation's operations "are fairly fluid and very organic."

Remmer says that in foundations like theirs, which are not connected to the family business and where the trustees all serve as volunteers, there is little tension because individual family members don't stand to gain monetarily. When family members are paid to run a foundation, however, it is particularly important to set policies and procedures, just as a family would for its business. As families bring the next generation into a foundation, it is also an important time to impose more structure on the operation. "You just have to turn it into a bit of an institution. If you don't do that, there could be a lot of misunderstanding," she cautions.

Policies and procedures for foundations should include a philanthropic mission, a code of ethics, conflict-of-interest policies, an investment policy, job descriptions for trustees, a discretionary grants policy (if they want family members to have certain amounts allocated for grants), and requirements and training for new trustees.

Remmer also advises term limits for trustees. She acknowledges, however, that the first generation is not likely to impose them on themselves because as creators of the foundation, they are inclined to stay on to provide guidance. As new trustees are added, the first generation realizes the need to enforce policies and procedures. Foundations, like businesses, are fluid and families should be open to new ideas from the next generation. "I believe you need to revisit your mission every five years to see if it is still relevant," Remmer says. "Most of the donors we work with are happy to have the next generation amend the mission." It could even change completely, Remmer says. "I'm guessing that when we open up our foundation to the next generation, it could change." She counsels founders who insist that their passion be carried out forever to take a realistic view by bringing in outside experts to achieve this instead of relying on family members. Remmer believes that the ideal family foundation is one that "serves both the family and society. It's a wonderful and exciting thing to be strategic, pick an area, and try to make a difference." According to Remmer, "Our family has not modified its mission statement for probably ten years, although we review it and modify our guidelines regularly. The criteria have changed at least once and the process is updated each year. It just turns out that this statement seems to work for us. We stay true to our mission and use it as a reminder that this is what we are about. In addition to printing it in our guidelines, I find myself using it when describing the foundation to potential grantees or partners."

The Remmer family mission statement and guidelines are shown below:

Typically, family foundations are specific in their goals, objective, guidelines, and funding procedures because the IRS monitors them. But whether families formalize their charitable intentions into a lasting legacy or choose to give informally, involving the entire family in the strategic plan will pay the most rewarding dividends in a family's spiritual connection.

REMMER FAMILY MISSION STATEMENT
AND GUIDELINES

MISSION

The mission of the Remmer Family Foundation is to reduce youth and female poverty by helping disadvantaged preadolescent and adolescent girls take charge of their own lives.

PROGRAM

The Remmer Family Foundation is a charitable foundation that makes grants to qualifying 501(c)(3) tax-exempt organizations. Currently, the Foundation is concentrating on applications from organizations located in the metropolitan Jacksonville, Florida, area and occasionally accepting those that are national in scope (e.g. research or advocacy).

The Foundation funds new and existing programs that strengthen girls and help them make good choices in their lives. We look for programs with the following qualities:

- Build on girls' strengths, thereby preventing problems that limit their opportunities.
- Focus on girls 9 to 15 years old.
- Address girls' needs in the context of family and community.
- Challenge girls, promote leadership abilities, and enable them to experience the satisfaction of achievement.
- Sensitive to and directly address issues of difference (e.g., class, race, culture) as strengths.

The Foundation also funds cutting-edge research on the development of girls. Most grants range from $5,000 to $15,000 and may be for one to three years. Awards given for more than one year will be subject to a careful annual review of grantee's performance.

APPLICATION PROCEDURE

In 2005, we will focus our grantmaking in Jacksonville, Florida, and will accept grant applications by invitation only. Due to our ongoing funding commitments, there will not be sufficient funds available to warrant an open application process. Please submit a proposal of no more than five pages, covering the following areas:

(Continued next page)

REMMER FAMILY MISSION STATEMENT
AND GUIDELINES (cont'd.)

- Mission, goals, and history of the organization.
- Rationale or need addressed by proposal.
- Objectives of proposal and approach for reaching objectives.
- Implementation plan and timeline.
- Indicators of success and approach for assessing success.
- Organization and project budgets.
- Other sources of funding.

We are a small family foundation, managed by our three volunteer trustees. We try to be as accessible and responsive as possible, but are not always successful. Please bear with us and be assured that we are interested in the extraordinary work that you do.

INDEX

About Bloomberg

BLOOMBERG L.P., founded in 1981, is a global information services, news, and media company. Headquartered in New York, the company has sales and news operations worldwide.

Bloomberg, serving customers on six continents, holds a unique position within the financial services industry by providing an unparalleled range of features in a single package known as the BLOOMBERG PROFESSIONAL® service. By addressing the demand for investment performance and efficiency through an exceptional combination of information, analytic, electronic trading, and Straight Through Processing tools, Bloomberg has built a worldwide customer base of corporations, issuers, financial intermediaries, and institutional investors.

BLOOMBERG NEWS®, founded in 1990, provides stories and columns on business, general news, politics, and sports to leading newspapers and magazines throughout the world. BLOOMBERG TELEVISION®, a 24-hour business and financial news network, is produced and distributed globally in seven languages. BLOOMBERG RADIO℠ is an international radio network anchored by flagship station BLOOMBERG® 1130 (WBBR-AM) in New York.

In addition to the BLOOMBERG PRESS® line of books, Bloomberg publishes *BLOOMBERG MARKETS*® magazine. To learn more about Bloomberg, call a sales representative at:

London:	+44-20-7330-7500
New York:	+1-212-318-2000
Tokyo:	+81-3-3201-8900

FOR IN-DEPTH MARKET INFORMATION AND NEWS, visit the Bloomberg website at www.bloomberg.com, which draws from the news and power of the BLOOMBERG PROFESSIONAL® service and Bloomberg's host of media products to provide high-quality news and information in multiple languages on stocks, bonds, currencies, and commodities.

About the Author

JUDY MARTEL, CFP®, is a vice president at Asset Management Advisors (AMA), a leading multifamily office and subsidiary of SunTrust Banks, Inc. Ms. Martel has twenty years of experience in journalism and public relations. She was a newspaper journalist for eleven years, and she has written extensively on wealth issues and family dynamics for such publications as *Robb Report Worth, Town & Country,* and *Vive* magazine, where she writes a regular column. She is a Certified Financial Planner™.

◦ ◦ ◦

The book's foreword is by James E. Hughes Jr., author of *Family Wealth: Keeping It in the Family* (Bloomberg Press). He brings to his foreword the perspective of a respected long-time family counselor and a pre-eminent expert in the field of family governance and wealth transfer.